THE EXISTENCE OF GOD

THE EXISTENCE

OF GOD

By Wallace I. Matson

ASSOCIATE PROFESSOR OF PHILOSOPHY
UNIVERSITY OF CALIFORNIA, BERKELEY

CORNELL UNIVERSITY PRESS

Ithaca, New York

Copyright © 1965 by Cornell University

All rights reserved

CORNELL UNIVERSITY PRESS

First published 1965
Second printing 1965
Third printing 1967

Library of Congress Catalog Card Number: 64-22946

PRINTED IN THE UNITED STATES OF AMERICA
BY VALLEY OFFSET, INC.
BOUND BY VAIL-BALLOU PRESS, INC.

To
Stephen Coburn Pepper

Acknowledgments

I AM grateful to the editorial staff of the Cornell University Press; to Professors Max Black, Terence Penelhum, David S. Shwayder, and Avrum Stroll, who criticized the whole of the manuscript at one stage or another; and to Professors Ernest W. Adams and Thomas S. Kuhn, who commented on certain parts. They have saved me from many blunders, factual, philosophical, and literary. Those that remain are due to my obstinacy.

W. M.

As to gods, I have no way of knowing whether or not there are any, or what they might be like. For many are the barriers to knowing: unclearness, and the shortness of man's life.

PROTAGORAS (ca. 450 B.C.)

If anyone says that the one and true God, our creator and lord, cannot be known with certainty with the natural light of human reason by means of the things that have been made: let him be anathema.

THE VATICAN COUNCIL (1870 A.D.)

Contents

Contents

Introduction

THE purpose of this book is to investigate the reasonableness of believing that there is at least one god. To that end we shall scrutinize all the important arguments the author has come upon that have been urged in support of this belief or against it. I shall try to conduct this investigation dispassionately and judiciously, as if we were arguing about the existence of the Himalayan Snowman, or the antineutrino.

Someone might object at the outset that there cannot be such a procedure, only a hypocritical pretense of it. For religion is not an intellectual system, but a general orientation to things, a way of life. To assume an air of detachment in scrutinizing the fundamental belief of religion is already to take a prejudicial stand, that of agnosticism or worse. Furthermore, since religion is a way of life, to adopt or reject it is to make an existential decision, and no one should be so naïve as to suppose that such decisions are products of dispassionate reasoning. How absurd to think that the existence of God can be investigated the way one might investigate the existence of the Himalayan Snowman! People do not *care* about the Snowman and the antineutrino the way they care about God:

not even if they are mountain climbers or physicists. The interest that such subjects may have is intellectual; it is properly satisfied by reading books. But no one ever said to himself: "I wonder whether there is a God? I hear Smith's book is the latest thing on the subject. They say he sets out the evidence most fairly, and evaluates the inferences quite dispassionately and judiciously. I had better read him before making up my mind." Natural theology, then, is frivolous and pointless; or else its real point is different from what it professes to be. The natural theologian does not reason, he rationalizes.

Such an objection is weighty, and the answer must concede much to it. Certainly God, as an object of human interest, is not on a par with anything else. A colleague of mine, when asked to appear as a representative of atheism in a panel discussion, replied that he was not enough interested in religion even to be an atheist. But such people presumably are rare, and in any case they will not read books on natural theology. A man is usually committed, one way or another, to religion, and rather early in life.

The real question is whether commitment on the part of author and reader necessarily precludes their engaging in rational discussion of the basis of their commitment. The obvious answer is that it makes discussion harder, but not impossible. There *can* be such a thing as dispassionate investigation of a matter that engages the passions of the disputants. Love may not have 20/20 vision, but it is not totally blind. Nor, for that matter, is hatred so many-eyed as the proverb tells us.

In politics, most Americans are committed Republicans or Democrats. Perhaps most of them prefer campaign biographies of their party leaders to candid and impartial portraits. It does not follow, however, that the audience for the latter consists exclusively of mugwumps. A loyal Democrat might prefer an account of Johnson as he really is to a piece of political hagiography. What is more, a loyal Democrat (or Republican) might write such an account. Likewise in religion it is not to be assumed without question that all believers and unbelievers prefer to believe or disbelieve with their eyes shut. In such a well-tilled field, the purpose of natural theology ought not to be considered that of changing anyone's mind, but rather of bringing to consciousness, in believer and unbeliever alike, the presuppositions and implications of belief and unbelief.

There is another important respect in which the question of the existence of God is unlike that of the existence of the Snowman and the antineutrino. In the latter cases, the evidence is not all in; however, we know what kind of evidence would be conclusive if found. The reverse is true in natural theology. Here it is safe to say that the evidence is already all in. Nobody is likely to turn up some new facts that would drastically strengthen or weaken the theistic hypothesis. Rather, the difficult questions are those concerned with what is to *count* as evidence for the conclusion: what kinds of inferences are to be regarded as legitimate for establishing, or conferring some probability on, the proposition that God exists. Roughly speaking: the difficulties in our inquiry will be with points of logic, not of fact.

Here the word "logic" is used in a broad sense. Our inquiry is into the reasonableness of believing that there is a god. Our main problem will be that of deciding what is to count as a reasonable belief in this context. Now there are at least three primary senses of "reasonable." Generally speaking, it is reasonable to believe in the existence of what presents itself as an object of experience. If, then, we have reason to believe that someone has had an experience such that a god *must* have been the object of that experience—if someone has *perceived* a god—then it is reasonable to believe that there is a god. Alternatively, if it can be shown that the proposition "God exists" follows deductively from self-evident (or at any rate highly plausible) premises, then it is shown at the same time that belief in the proposition is reasonable in an accepted primary sense of "reasonable," namely the mathematical. And if the proposition is an explanatory hypothesis confirmed by the weight of relevant factual evidence (as electrons explain the observed phenomena of electricity, though nobody has ever seen an electron), the conclusion is reasonable in the scientific sense. We shall not assume however, that these three senses—the perceptual, the mathematical, and the natural-scientific—are the only proper senses of "reasonable." It has been argued that the existence of God is provable neither deductively nor inductively, yet belief in God is reasonable. We shall not ignore these arguments in our discussion. In particular, we shall not ignore the variations on the theme "The heart has its reasons, that Reason knows nothing of."

The Order of the Inquiry

As it is not likely that new facts will be discovered with important bearing on the theistic hypothesis, neither is it probable that radically new arguments in support of it will be developed. In about three millennia of speculation, the ingenuity of apologists has sufficed to produce only half a dozen or so such arguments. (This fact is no reflection on theologians; we shall find grounds to support the conclusion that this array is exhaustive—that new arguments are in principle impossible.) The order in which we consider them is of no great importance; I have adopted one that seems natural and convenient, as follows:

We shall begin, as most people do in fact, with *authority* as the basis of belief in God. We shall consider what there is to be said for and against the views that it is reasonable to believe that there is a god on the ground that the antiquity and universality of the belief is a guarantee of its truth; or on the ground that its truth is vouched for by a person or persons of such extraordinary character that he or they could not be mistaken.

It should be fairly clear at the outset that even if authority is enough to justify belief in a god, there ought to be non-authoritarian grounds also. The investigation will then shift to scrutiny of reasons that are alleged to be compelling in themselves.

Nonauthoritarian belief might be reasonable because it is the outcome of *experience*. The kinds of experience that might suffice are indefinite in number, but they are either like ordinary sense experiences (visions and voices), or radically unlike them (mystical illumination).

Rational conviction may also be based on argument. Here we shall review three traditional proofs of the existence of God: the ontological argument, the cosmological (or first cause) argument, and the argument from design.

At this point we shall have completed our scrutiny of considerations urged in support of the reasonableness of belief in God in the ordinary sense of "reasonable," i.e., shown to be certainly or probably *true*. We shall not be finished, however, for there remains the pragmatic argument, the contention that theistic belief is reasonable because of its good effects. The alleged good effects may be individual well-being, support of morality, or stability of social institutions.

Definition of Terms

To avoid getting into the "I see—*your* God is *my* Devil" predicament, let us specify the meanings to be assigned (until further notice) to three key terms: "deity," "God," and "god."

The word "deity" will mean personal, superhuman, active, and powerful intelligence. To qualify as an active and powerful intelligence, a being must be capable of forming and executing purposes; and he must, at least on occasion, exercise this function. Since not only men but even some beasts are active and powerful intelligences in this sense, the requirement is added that the being be superhuman; though it is difficult to specify exactly what it is to be superhuman. I do not want to make it part of this minimum definition that a deity must by definition be more intelligent, or more powerful, than any human being; I want to leave open the possibility that there might be a deity whom merely human ingenuity and resources could aid or thwart. Arbitrarily, let us specify that a superhuman intelligence must be capable of fully understanding at least one human language. The requirement of personality has the purpose of ruling out of our discussion pantheism, the doctrine of karma, and the use of "god" as a collective term or metaphor for individually human intelligences, emotions, or what not.

A deity, in this sense, may (but need not) be infinite in some respect. A deity might be born and die. A deity might have been active at some time, but now be retired. He might have superiors. His activity might be limited to this planet, or even to a particular region of it. He might be relatively stupid (but not an utter idiot). He might be virtuous or wicked. Needless to say, a deity might be male or female or sexless. Examples of deities are: Jupiter, Moloch, Huitzilopochtli, Aladdin's genie, the Archangel Gabriel, Diana of the Ephesians, Madame Pelée, Satan, (possibly) poltergeists.

"God," on the other hand, will signify infinite Being—infinite in the respects of knowledge and wisdom, power and goodness. Theologians deduce from the concept of infinite Being that there can be no more than one such Being; that He must be spiritual and incorporeal; self-existent, i.e., without beginning or end—indeed, timeless; immutable; and the source and support of all finite being. These properties are hereby incorporated into the definition.

I shall use the word "god" (small g) to mean "God or deity," in contexts where it is not necessary to specify which of the two is meant.

As these terms have been defined, God has all the characteristics of a deity; so that if it is reasonable to believe that God exists, then it is reasonable to believe that there is a god (deity)—but not (necessarily) conversely. Monotheism is to be understood as the doctrine that God exists; consequently it is not contradictory to say that monotheism is true, and at the same time that there is more than one god, provided the other deities do not and cannot, so to speak, get in the way.

Part I

AUTHORITY
AND EXPERIENCE

Authority

MOST of us learned by being burned that fire burns, and that the earth is round by being told. Whatever we know we learn at first by finding out for ourselves or from authority, though what we first learn from teachers we may later confirm from our experience.

Statistically, authority vastly preponderates as the source of the beliefs of every human being. This predominance is the greater, the more educated the person is. Authority forms chains: I believe that the earth is round because my teacher told me so, and she believed it because her teacher said so, and so on back. Nor is there anything deplorable about this; we should be ignorant indeed if we knew nothing but what we had found out for ourselves. Our superiority to the brute creation is due mostly to these authority-chains, which language makes possible.

In general, it is reasonable to believe what one is told. But not always—as everyone finds out for himself and learns from authorities also. It is clear that one requirement for the reasonableness of belief in authority is that the chain should somewhere be anchored: someone along the line must have discovered it for himself. Sebastián del Cano found that the earth was round by sailing around it; before him Aristotle, and before Aristotle the Pythagorean mathematicians, had reasons, though less conclusive ones, for the belief. There cannot be an endless regress of authorities.

Or can there? In the course of our investigation, we shall more than once come to a point where we are urged to believe something on the ground that to deny it would result in our getting into an infinite regress ("There must be a first cause, because otherwise . . ."); and sometimes we shall retort that this is nothing to worry about ("After all, what is wrong with supposing that this is the effect of that, and that is the effect of t'other, and so on ad infinitum?"). For this reason we should give some consideration to the possibility that to believe that God exists may be reasonable just because the belief is so ancient and so widespread.

The Argument from General Consent

The argument we refer to is this: whatever has been believed always, everywhere, and by all is true. Now all peoples, everywhere and always, have believed that there is a god. Therefore there is a god.

We must use the small g, because no one could maintain that God has been so universally believed in. Nevertheless, to prove that there is a god is to make some progress toward showing that God exists.

Not, however, that much progress is going to be made here. For the minor premise of the argument is factually false (witness Buddhists, Jains, agnostics and atheists in our own culture), and the major premise hardly commends itself as a principle of reasoning (was the earth in olden times flat and motionless?). Nor are we any longer in the grip of the feeling that underlies the argument and that presumably once gave it plausibility—the feeling that we must have faith in the doctrines of the ancients, for they knew more than we do.

All the same, the argument is not a total loss. The minor premise is *almost* true; if rephrased so as to refer not to gods specifically but to religion, it may be impeccable. And the major premise has at least the force of indicating that the burden of proof lies on the denier of a universally held belief. If there should be no reason at all to believe that there is a god, and also no reason at all to believe that there is not, then the fact that the overwhelming majority of mankind believe there *is* would in itself furnish a reasonable ground for the belief. Or, if that seems arbitrary, one might say that other things being equal, a universally held belief is presumed to have survival value; and since in general whatever has survival value conforms to reality, the presumption is that such a belief is true. The fate of the universal belief about the shape of the earth reminds us, however, that the presumption is rebuttable. We shall consider these matters further in Part IV.

The Argument from Miracles

It is too soon, however, to conclude that a chain of authorities must be anchored in reasons open to everybody's inspection. We must first consider the possibility that there might be a self-justifying or absolute authority. Might it conceivably be reasonable to believe someone who asserts, "There is a god," not because of any arguments he produces, but because he has such a character that he is obviously worthy of credence in such matters?

Ordinary experts on various subjects are not self-justifying authorities in this sense. One often takes what they say on trust, without requiring them to back up their assertions with reasons. More than that, the expert-layman contrast implies that the expert, if challenged by the layman to justify his assertions, will, in at least some cases, not be able to make those reasons intelligible to the layman. But it is assumed that if the expert cannot make himself understood to everyone, at any rate he can be checked up on by other experts; more importantly, any layman of a certain level of intelligence could put himself into a position to check for himself, if he went to the trouble. In contrast to this, we are now asking whether there might be some expert who asserts that there is a god; who does not or cannot produce any reasons which an ordinary person could check, even in principle; and who is such that nevertheless it is reasonable to believe him, even in the absence of any reasons other than his say-so.

Such a person would have to be extraordinary, in a certain sense superhuman. Now the capacities of men can be divided into the intellectual, the moral, and the physical. Extraordinary moral capabilities—extreme goodness, saintliness—could not of themselves validate the person's claim; the human situation is not so desperate that moral impeccability—resistance to all sorts of temptations, perfect kindness and love —is self-evidently beyond mere human nature. To be sure, a perfectly virtuous man would have to be perfectly truthful. It does not follow, though, that if he said, "There is a god," there would have to be a god. The moral virtue of truthfulness consists in saying nothing that one does not believe; but a virtuous man may believe what is false.

One can imagine intellectual powers of such a high order that a presumption might be raised against the possibility of their being the fulfillment of merely human potentialities. We can imagine someone really able to do what fortunetellers and clairvoyants pretend to do; who in addition could prove Fermat's last theorem, solve the four-color problem. set up an experiment to demonstrate the existence of the gravitational particle, and so on *ad lib*. Should such a person claim to know that there is a god of any sort, including God, it would be reasonable to take him seriously; the more so, if he were also extraordinarily saintly.

Mere display of unusual physical powers—wonder-working —may seem, in this century, rather vulgar and inappropriate to establishing claims about the supernatural, no matter what previous ages may have thought. Perhaps most philosophers today would say that demonstrated ability to "violate physical laws" could show only that the laws of nature are not what we thought they were, or in the extreme case, that determinism is false, that some events do not have causes. Be that as it may, if someone proved able to walk on water, fly through the air, sail a steamship by cooling the ocean, restore partially decomposed bodies to life, etc.; and if we knew he was really doing them, not hoaxing us or inducing hallucinations (it would be difficult to know this, but not, I think, in principle impossible), then surely a point would be reached where it would be sheerest dogmatism to dismiss his claim to be a nature-controller, i.e., a god or some god's ambassador extraordinary. There is, however, a limit on what such wonder-working could establish: no matter what its manifestations, it could never prove, nor even render probable, the existence of God; for whatever he did would be compatible with the hypothesis that the nature-controller was not identical with the nature-creator, and moreover, that the nature-controller's powers had *some* limits: a claim to infinite powers could not be validated in any finite set of acts. But in combination with extraordinary moral and intellectual powers, these superhuman physical manifestations should suffice to make it reasonable (or at least not unreasonable) to give credence to the expert's assertion of the existence of God.

The modern reader may be surprised and offended to find

7

that I am defending the cogency of the argument from miracles. Let me state to what extent I am defending that argument and to what extent not.

First, I am arguing that the existence of a *deity* might conceivably be confirmed by miracles. (It is only an uninteresting verbal point whether we should call the expert, about whom we have been romancing, a deity or a superman.) Second, I think it is conceivable that a person might possess such miraculous powers—including, especially, miraculous insight into the nature of things—that some degree of rational credibility would attach to his assertion of the existence of God, even in the absence of any other reason for believing in such a Being. But I am not arguing that the existence of a God has ever been established, or rendered probable in the least degree, by such means.

We have been talking only about what might conceivably happen. Any person who says that such an expert exists or has existed must back up his allegation with evidence, consisting of his own testimony that he has confronted the expert, or of the testimony of other ordinary mortals. Here the rule enunciated by Hume in his celebrated essay on miracles[1] applies: such testimony would be rationally credible only if it would be more miraculous for the witnesses to be deceived or deceiving than for the events in question to have occurred as described; and even then we should be setting one miracle against another, so that the result would be "mutual annihilation and suspense of judgment." If anyone thinks Hume's requirement too severe, he must admit at least that very high standards of credibility—in respect of disinterest, sophistication, and lack of influence by crowd contagion—should be imposed on the witnesses, of whom there should be a large

[1] David Hume, *An Enquiry concerning Human Understanding* (1748), sec. 10, "Of Miracles."

number in tolerable unanimity. It is a matter of historical fact that such conditions have never been satisfied for testimony concerning any candidate for our position of expert on the reality of a god. In short: even assuming that A is such an expert, it would be extremely difficult for B (an ordinary mortal) to make sure he was confronted with such an expert (for B, if rational, should be aware of the manifold possibilities of his being deceived); and difficult *in excelsis* for C to believe in A on the testimony of B, or of several B's. The requisite conditions for such rational credibility have never been satisfied.

Our general conclusion is that there could be circumstances in which it would be reasonable to believe in the existence of a deity, or possibly even of God, on the basis of someone's say-so alone; but that no one, at present, is in those circumstances; nor does anyone, at present, have any reason to believe that anyone else has ever been so situated.

Before we leave this subject, we should point out in fairness that the argument from miracles has seldom if ever been relied on to *establish* the claim that there is a god. Rather, miracles have been offered as corroborative evidence for theism, and to provide credentials for particular persons as spokesmen of gods antecedently and independently supposed to exist; or to give evidence of the greater power of one god as compared with another. There does not appear to be anything in principle improper about such procedures. Supposing there to be a personal nature-controller, it would be rather odd if he did not from time to time manifest that power in some striking and unusual way, to accomplish some good purpose. Perhaps one might even argue that nonoccurrence of miracles is evidence *against* the existence of a nature-controller; but we shall not pursue this line of thought.

Experience

IN human affairs generally, the notion of a self-justifying authority is not admitted; and we have seen that there is no reason to make an exception in religious matters. Now we can begin to consider reasons, offered as justifying belief in gods, that are at least on their face of the same sort as reasons granted by everyone to be good reasons in other contexts.

One kind of good reason for believing in the existence of X is that one has perceived X, one has had experience of X. To be sure, philosophers sometimes question, or write as if they were questioning, the cogency of such reasons. Some theorists of knowledge profess to find many difficulties in justifying belief in the existence of a tree "in reality," "out there," "independent of the perceiver" merely on the ground that normal persons truthfully report that they see, smell, kick, climb in, or cut down a tree. I shall, however, ignore all such skeptical cavils and take it for granted that seeing or smelling a tree is normally a good reason for believing that an "objective" tree exists ("normally" meaning: in the absence of special positive reasons for doubt, such as ingestion of drugs, paresis, crazy-house context, hypnotist in vicinity, etc.); that a certain recognizable and distinguishable taste—the "taste of gin"—is normally a good reason for believing there to be gin in the punch; that objects roughly similar to ourselves in appearance and behavior are also like us in possessing consciousnesses with roughly similar contents; in a word, I shall assume, naively if you like, that perception is in general valid ground for claiming knowledge, at the same time remaining aware, as everyone must, of the existence of illusions and delusions, and of the difficulty, in some cases, of distinguishing the veridical from the illusory.[2]

Perception

We need to indicate, however, how it is that we distinguish between perceptions and other kinds of conscious or quasi-conscious experiences, such as feeling blue, having a toothache, and dreaming. Now some philosophers do not make a distinction here; they speak of "perceiving one's toothache," "perceiving a red patch" (tomato or afterimage alike), and "perceiving a pink elephant [or maybe elephantoid patch] chasing one in a dream." Although I believe that there are objections to this way of speaking which are more than merely verbal ones, this is not the place to argue the point.

The verb "perceive" is transitive, and takes as its grammatical object only a "that" clause or the name of a thing—usually physical, but we shall allow the possibility of its being mental, or if you prefer, spiritual—that is independent of the perceiver. Thus it is not correct to speak of perceiving pains, afterimages, and pink elephants. It is all right to say, "I *thought* I perceived a pink elephant (but of course I had

[2] I do not intend, however, to make the concession implied in the word "assume." There is no reason to doubt the validity, in general, of perception. See J. L. Austin, *Sense and Sensibilia* (Oxford: Clarendon Press, 1962).

delirium tremens at the time)," "I seemed to hear the door-bell (but I was mistaken; it was a ringing in the ear)," "the beamish boy perceived a jabberwock whiffling through the tulgey wood" (where the context indicates that the assertion is not to be taken as literally describing a fact).

One does not perceive qualities per se: "I saw something red" will do, but not "I saw red," except as a metaphor; nor the philosophical jargon "I saw a red patch," unless this is a description, say, of a feature of someone's shirt. ("Lemon juice is sour, though nothing is a sour taste."—Kotarbinski.[3]) Whether it is possible to perceive ghoulies and ghosties and things that go bump in the night, turns on the factual question of whether such entities are or are not part of the furniture of the universe, with their own careers, independent of the anxieties of Scotsmen.

Seeing, hearing, tasting, smelling, and touching are kinds of perceiving, but there may be others. "Extrasensory perception" is not here assumed to be a contradiction in terms. In our usage it is a hypothesis, not a matter of definition, that every case of perception involves a process in a sense receptor.

Perception is analyzable into a conscious experience (CE) of a perceiver (P), the object (O) perceived, and a relation (R) between the object and the perception. The CE must reveal characters that the O really has. To defend this statement, or even to explain it fairly fully, would involve us in unnecessary complications. An example may help to convey the bearing of this requirement: a tomato really is red. Someone looks at a tomato in a darkroom (under a red light). If he follows our recommendations, he will not say, "I saw a white tomato," but rather, "I seemed to see a white tomato,"

[3] Tadeusz Kotarbinski, "The Fundamental Ideas of Pansomatism," *Mind*, LXIV (1955), 494.

or "The tomato looked white," i.e., "The experience I had was like what I would have had if, in normal illumination, I had seen a tomato that really was white."

R is a causal relation. O causes CE or is an indispensable part of the cause. If I have my eyes closed and experience a hallucination of a tomato in a dish, I am not perceiving a tomato, even if there happens to be a tomato in a dish in front of me.

To sum up these points, perception, as we shall use the word, requires a real object. This is the important distinction between it and two other kinds of conscious experiences: feelings and fantasies. "Feelings" are experiences which do not, in and of themselves, reveal any features of the outside world, and which are such that no one is tempted to suppose that they do: aches and pains, joy, anger are some examples. Of course it is not denied that one is often led to infer features of the outside world from feelings; and such inferences are often justified. From "seeing stars" we may infer a lump on the head; but "seeing stars" is not perceiving a lump on the head, any more than it is perceiving stars, or perceiving anything at all. "Fantasies" will here be employed as a general term for all conscious experiences that are similar (in form and content) to perceptions, and that it is natural to describe in the "It seemed as if I were perceiving . . ." locution, or in terms limited in their application to such experiences: "I dreamed that . . . ," "I pictured to myself the . . . ," "I imagined myself to be . . . ," etc. We subdivide fantasies into the subclasses of imaginings, those fantasies which the subject does not confuse with perception; and delusions, which the subject mistakes for perception.

Nothing is a perception that does not fulfill our conditions of revelation and causality. It is of course one of the major traditional problems of philosophy to develop criteria for knowing that these conditions are satisfied—for distinguishing, and knowing that one has distinguished, between perceptions and delusions. This is another morass that we shall skirt. Or at any rate we shall not wade in it more deeply than we have to.

Visions and Voices

We now return to our main problem, that of trying to determine what sort of experience might suffice to certify the existence of a god.

Experiences that might possibly accomplish this will either be like ordinary experiences or unlike them. Let us consider the former class first.

A god-certifying experience might be like a perception; indeed, it might even *be* a perception. Let us assume that someone is known to have perceived some person and the perceiver claims, on the basis of this experience, to have knowledge of the existence of a god.

The claim, if reasonable, must be based either on some reasons advanced by the allegedly divine personage perceived or on the character of the personage. We have already considered the latter case, and we have only to repeat our conclusion: very extraordinary behavior by the personage might confer some probability on the claim; but there is no convincing evidence of this ever having happened. The evidential value (if any) of such epiphanies is in confirming beliefs otherwise established, whether in the first instance rationally or not; but if the original belief was not based on rational considerations, the appearance cannot confer reasonableness on it.

But is not something more than superfluous corroboration to be expected from an appearance of a well-known personage of religion? For surely this would show that the personage in question was real, not merely mythical. Suppose that belief in god X is based on an ancient document, which among other assertions minutely describes Y, the immortal messenger of X. Suppose now that a being of precisely this description (there is not and could not be any mistake about it) appears out of nowhere and announces that he is Y, sent by X; after performing various miracles, he vanishes upward. Would this not confirm the claims of the document?

Of course it would. To say so, however, is not to concede any more than we have already admitted in discussing miracles. The tremendous, if not insuperable, difficulties of ruling out the possibility of hallucination would remain. The evidential value of an epiphany would be greatly increased if Y appeared to someone who had never heard of him or of the document in question. It is safe to say that there is no reason to suppose that any such Y (or X, for that matter) has ever appeared to anyone who had not previously heard of Y or X. There are famous instances of apparitions to *nonbelievers*, but this does not alter the case: the psychology of such phenomena is well enough understood. So far from anyone *knowing* that someone has perceived a supernatural personage, there is no reason to believe that it has ever occurred. For the ordinary tests for distinguishing perceptions from fantasies turn on the publicity of the phenomena. (It will be noted that no publicity requirement has been incorporated into our definition of perception.) If P reports that he sees or hears something of a size or loudness such that ordinary persons normally see and hear such things, and no one else in the vicinity sees it or hears it, the claim of perception is dismissed without further ado. A certain degree of corroboration by others, however, may be attained without validating the claim, because of the well-known phenomena of mass delusion. What is needed is that several persons, of normal eyesight, hearing, and intelligence, not predisposed to believe reports of the phenomenon, and so insulated from one another that the effects of suggestibility can be ruled out, should corroborate the apparition. There may be some reason to believe that such corroboration has been achieved for some "paranormal" manifestations investigated by psychical researchers. However, such evidence does not seem to be available to support any claim for the existence of a god, except at most a very inferior sort of deity (poltergeists and such). We can imagine what the evidence would be like that would support the sort of claim that we are interested in; but in fact such evidence does not exist. This is not to say that it may not be discovered in future; I am inclined to agree with C. D. Broad[4] that theologians should be more interested in psychical research than they are.

To be sure, failure of publicity tests does not disprove the claim that an apparition of a god or his messenger is a perception. We have defined "perception" in such a way that if experience reveals certain characters of a being, and that being really exists and has those characters, and, furthermore, the being causes the subject to have the experience, then the experience is a perception. Publicity is only the most usual and reliable way in which we test whether the experience is of this nature. But as we have just pointed out, an experience may pass the test and still not be a perception; equally it might fail the test and still really be a perception. This possibility has to be seriously considered in the religious context, and perhaps in no other. For a god—a nature-controller, hence a perception-controller—might see fit to reveal himself selectively: just to the believer, or to the virtuous, or to the infidel in need of shock therapy; never to those whose hearts he had hardened or to those beyond some pale or other. In-

[4] C. D. Broad, *Religion, Philosophy and Psychical Research* (New York: Harcourt, Brace & Co., 1953), p. 236.

deed, we can even imagine that such behavior might not be a matter of choice on the part of the god; it might be a law of nature or of supernature that a god of limited power could not "get through" except to those already somehow attuned to him. Such hypotheses would explain why A sees him and B does not, compatibly with A's really seeing him.

If that is the way some god chooses to behave, however, he does so at the price of depriving his epiphanies of evidential value. He really appears to A, we suppose; even so, A cannot know that he has been favored with a theophany, for in the absence of confirmation from fellow men, the hypothesis that the appearance is delusory must have greater probability than that it is veridical. And even if A somehow did know (was rationally convinced of) the reality of the phenomenon, there still could be no reason for B to accept A's testimony concerning it.

The case is different if there is independent evidence for the existence of a god. In that case, there might be some probability, on that evidence, that the god would manifest himself, perhaps privately; and there could be ways of distinguishing genuine manifestations from spurious ones. To perceive the god, or his messengers, would then be to have confirmatory evidence for the existence of that god. But it seems equally clear that no such phenomena—no visions or voices—could ever of themselves establish, or confer the slightest degree of probability on, the existence of a god, either for the recipient of the visitation or for anyone else. (We have noted the one possible exception to this verdict: manifestation to someone utterly ignorant of the supposed existence of the god in question.) Unless the existence of the god is first established by some other means, there is not and cannot be any reason to believe that a private appearance of that god is not a delusion.

Mystical Experience

WE must now see how the case stands with experiences unlike ordinary perceptions. At the outset it may seem clear that if epiphanies cannot establish the existence of gods, then experiences not involving personal appearances must be of even less evidential value. For an experience unlike a perception must either be a feeling—and we need not labor the point that a mere feeling or hunch, not confirmed or substantiated by something else, is without evidential value according to the ordinary canons of evidence—or else it must be something altogether unlike any ordinary experience. Now one trouble with apparitions is their privacy; but at least the nature of the experience can be communicated to others. One can say, "The being was of such and such form and figure, and he spake thus and so." But if an experience is utterly unlike any that one's audience has undergone, then one cannot even describe it intelligibly. It is hard to imagine what evidential value an indescribable encounter might have to others.

To others. . . . But what about to the person who has it? We must consider these two cases separately.

Let us try to rid ourselves of prejudices. Let us try to determine in advance and in a vacuum, so to speak, what a direct experience of a god should be like; what would be the most "natural" (in some sense) form for such an encounter to take; and let us try to forget what we have heard already on this score.

Now God is totally unlike any object of our ordinary experience; and if it is allowable to speak of God as a sort of limiting case that finite deities might more or less approximate, then insofar as a deity approaches to the character of God just to that extent the deity moves farther and farther from the orbit of worldly doings. Just to that extent, also, the deity becomes interesting as a religious object, a fit object of worship. But likewise, just to the extent to which a deity is unlike an everyday object, so one should expect in advance that an encounter with him would be unlike an everyday encounter. Hence the presumption is that an immediate experience of God, or of any august deity, would be so very strange as to be partly or wholly indescribable.

Of course religious persons of a certain degree of sophistication realize this; that is why, if they put any credence at all in epiphanies, they take it for granted that the appearance is only of a messenger (*angellos*) of the god, not of the god himself. On the other hand, it is equally clear that the mere occurrence of an indescribable experience cannot be regarded, in advance, as evidence for the existence of a god or of anything else. And it is hard to see how one indescribable experience can be distinguished from another—at all events by one who only hears tell of such occurrences. It looks then as if an experience, to be evidence for the existence of a god, must be indescribable; but an indescribable experience cannot be evidence for anything; therefore no experience can be evidence for the existence of a god.

It is, however, only the spectator who is at this impasse.

Possibly the man who has the experience is not thus embarrassed, and perhaps there is some way in which he can communicate something of evidential value to the spectator.

Experiences of a unique and indescribable sort, which are taken by their subjects to be revelatory of a god, are not very common; but they are common enough to have a name, "mystical experiences"; and they are reported in nearly all cultures. We shall use the term "mystic" to refer to the subject of such an experience. This usage should not be confused with the vaguer, usually derogatory, popular sense.

Although the content of the mystical experience is indescribable, this does not mean that the experience itself cannot be characterized. William James lists four properties:

1. *Ineffability.* . . . The subject of it immediately says that it defies expression, that no adequate report of its contents can be given in words. . . .

2. *Noetic quality.*—Although so similar to states of feeling, mystic states seem to those who experience them to be also of knowledge. They are states of insight into depths of truth unplumbed by the discursive intellect. They are illuminations, revelations, full of significance and importance, all inarticulate though they remain; and as a rule they carry with them a curious sense of authority for aftertime. . . .

3. *Transiency.*—Mystical states cannot be sustained for long. Except in rare instances, half an hour, or at most an hour or two, seems to be the limit beyond which they fade into the light of common day. . . .

4. *Passivity.*—Although the oncoming of mystical states may be facilitated by preliminary voluntary operations . . . when the characteristic sort of consciousness once has set in, the mystic feels as if his own will were in abeyance, and indeed sometimes as if he were grasped and held by a superior power.[5]

[5] William James, *The Varieties of Religious Experience* (New York and London: Longmans, Green, 1902), Lect. XVI, pp. 380 f.

The ineffability of the mystical experience has not prevented the creation of a vast and fascinating mystical literature, in which mystics attempt to convey the feel of their experiences, and to state those insights into the nature of things that they say have been revealed to them.

First, mystics pretty generally agree that their experiences reveal the reality of an order of being distinct from, and in some sense higher than, the world perceived through the senses. Commonly the world of the senses is inferred to be mere confused appearance of this higher reality, or at any rate dependent on it.

Second, reality is revealed to be one; at all events, it is more accurately described as one than as many, though no description is quite right. In any case, reality is emphatically not the "one damned thing after another" that the average sensual man supposes it to be. Moreover, the unity of all things is a tighter unity than any mere regularity or fitting together of parts that science may discover. The unity revealed to the mystics (we are told) transcends the categories of subject and object altogether. The mystic, in his rapture, does not contemplate the unity of all things; he is absorbed into it.

Third, reality is perfect. All that is ultimately valuable is somehow embedded in it; all that is evil is somehow excluded, as "mere appearance" or what you will. Optimism seems to be universal among mystics—even among the Oriental mystics, whose view of the world of the senses is gloomy indeed. And that is just as one would expect: for whatever religion may be, certainly it is supposed to offer us some sort of deliverance from, compensation for, or means of coming to terms with the uneasinesses and horrors that permeate the ordinary condition of man in nature.

Finally, the human soul is identical with, or at least akin

to, the supersensible reality. Whatever may be the status of the material world, the soul, or at least some part or aspect of it, is of the same stuff as ultimate reality. Hence it is capable of shuffling off its mortal coil, of escaping from its fleshly prison, and of experiencing the ultimate bliss of reabsorption into the Infinite. The mystical experience itself is usually interpreted as a temporary foretaste of the heavenly state.

These four insights seem to comprise the principal points of agreement found in mystics of different cultures. Within a particular culture or religious tradition, a more specific consensus may obtain, for instance, concerning the reality of the Holy Trinity; and such conclusions may be different from, even incompatible with, what mystics of other religious antecedents infer from their ecstasies. From this fact some critics are led to deny that there is any mystical unanimity, hence to explain away mystical experience as delusion, in effect the heroic degree of wishful thinking. Now certainly mystics do agree on some points and disagree on others; to a certain extent it is an arbitrary matter whether one emphasizes the agreements and explains away the disagreements or vice versa. But it is too much to expect that thousands of human beings, vastly separated in space and time, each with his own cultural and religious heritage, each being the subject of an experience of such a nature as not to be describable in any ordinary language, let alone translatable into all the others—it is too much to expect that all these men should agree on every plank of a metaphysical platform, that their separate interpretations of their separate experiences should be unmixed with circumambient ideas. Rather, any substantial agreement at all will take on an extraordinary and striking importance.

That many mystics, probably a majority, are in substantial agreement on the four points that we have sketched, seems to be a fact; at any rate we shall assume that it is. This is a fact, then, to be explained. The agreement goes very far toward canceling the suspicions otherwise aroused by the private and ineffable nature of the experience. One hypothesis to explain the agreement—a hypothesis that it would be sheer dogmatism to dismiss with no consideration—is that the mystics happen to be right.

Is it our business, however, to investigate the claims of mystics? For our study is of reasons for believing that there is a god; and mystics are not in agreement on the proposition. The existence of God, as an Infinite Personal Intelligence, is not part of the mystical consensus, which seems to point to a view that is more akin to pantheism than to the personal theism that we are scrutinizing. Mystical ecstasy is often described as union with a something—call it X; but more often than not this X is described as impersonal (or superpersonal, if that is different), as something identical with the whole of reality.

However, the relation of God to the world is a nice point in any theology; and it surely is not our business to dwell on the subtleties of that relation. Moreover, our study will be naive and trivial unless we emancipate ourselves from the crudities of anthropomorphism; yet one of the prices of the emancipation is the giving up of any comfortable, intuitive notion of personality, as the term is to be applied to God. All that clearly remains is some abstract notion of unity; and mysticism is surely not wanting in such a notion. In any case, many mystics (suspiciously, those reared in theistic cultures) agree that the experience reveals the existence of God, in a more or less orthodox sense of the proposition. We cannot therefore excuse ourselves from the task of looking into the bearing of their experience on our question.

It will simplify our study if we make certain assumptions. Let us assume that all the mystics we are to consider are unanimous in asserting that God—infinitely powerful, wise, and good Being, the source and support of all creation—exists. When asked for their reasons, they tell us that they know this with absolute certainty because the mystical experience has revealed it to them in such a manner that no doubt whatever is admissible. But when pressed further, they lapse into silence and only smile.

The nonmystic is put into an exasperating situation. Here he is being solicited to adopt an exotic metaphysic, on no better evidence than the say-so of certain persons who claim to have reasons, but who decline altogether to produce them, saying that language—which is adequate enough to describe quantum theory and relativity—is incapable of expressing those reasons. It is understandable if the nonmystic's reaction is to complain that the mystic is crazy. And evidence tending to support this conclusion is not difficult to find. The claim to possess a profound but inexpressible insight is characteristic of many psychotic states. The austerities and mortifications practiced by many mystics in order to "facilitate the oncoming of mystical states" might be interpreted as systematic methods for driving oneself out of one's mind. The mystic ecstasy itself, as far as an outsider can judge, bears a sinister resemblance to intoxications that can be induced by drugs known to be deleterious to the higher nervous functions. It is well known that in many cultures drug-induced hallucinations are ritually cultivated; and it is not clear how, or even whether, these states are to be distinguished from true mystic ecstasy. It is somehow unseemly that the secret of the universe should be unveiled via eating mushrooms.

The mystic retorts that it is outrageous to suppose that men like Plato, St. Paul, Plotinus, and Pascal, and women like St. Theresa, were simply demented. In rebuttal the skeptic speaks of the proverbial thin line and points out that no one with even a superficial acquaintance with the great of the world, particularly the intellectually great, is under the illusion that they are as a class paradigms of mental health. The counter-rebuttal is that the great mystics were great poets, philosophers, scientists, even administrators, because of their mysticism and not in spite of it. The beatific vision is a source of strength as well as of joy. Counter-counterrebuttal: various neuroses (if not psychoses) often have the effect of making their sufferers into most energetic and creative persons.

And so it goes. It might appear that the controversy could be resolved if more detailed clinical material were collected. There is, however, a more fundamental difficulty. Sanity must presumably be defined in terms of adjustment to reality; and the question here is, precisely, what *is* reality? If it is the everyday world, and only that, then pretty clearly the mystic is insane, temporarily or permanently. But to decide the issue this way would obviously beg the question.

We shall just leave the matter up in the air. Mysticism, for all we know, may be lunacy; and the ravings of lunatics, we may assume, are of no evidential value for any purpose except diagnosis. It is not unreasonable to suspect that mysticism is insanity. What is unreasonable is to conclude, in the present state of our knowledge, that it must be. In consequence, we are obliged to explore the hypothesis that mystics are sane.

In that case, their conviction must be taken seriously, as the firm belief of reasonable men arrived at on the basis of evidence available to them. And if they are being reasonable in believing, is it not reasonable for the nonmystics to share their belief on trust?

It may seem at this point that our answer must be negative, because the situation is identical with that of the absolute authority, which we have already rejected as a source of rational belief. But it is not, though the difference is subtle. The absolute authority urges us to believe him just because he is who he is, and for no other reason. The mystic, however, urges us to believe him because his belief is grounded in satisfactory evidence—though he cannot tell us what that evidence is. There is a real difference here, because if the existence of evidence is not even mentioned, then the question of possible access to it does not arise. But when the assertion is made that some kind of evidence exists, then it may after all prove possible to get access to it: the nonmystic may be given directions for becoming a mystic; or failing this, there may be some indirect method of establishing, by ordinary means, the existence and relevance of the evidence.

Physicists tell us that pi-mesons exist. This kind of assertion, and the evidence offered for it, may be taken as a paradigm case of objective existence ("out there"), public verifiability, inferences drawn from undoubted facts in accordance with impeccable canons of scientific procedure, and all the rest that the nonmystic charges the mystic with ignoring. For all that, the evidence for the existence of the pi-meson is in fact inaccessible to the author of this book and very likely to most of its readers. Indeed, the meaning of the sentence "There are pi-mesons" is not understood. The author takes it on faith that this sentence has a meaning to those who concern themselves with such matters and that evidence of its truth is available to them.

It is surely reasonable for me (and for you) to do this. It would be impertinent for us to say: "The alleged evidence for pi-mesons is the property of a small confraternity, who make no pretense of communicating it to anyone outside their clique. What imposture!" For the physicists' retort is unanswerable: "To be sure, the evidence for pi-mesons is in fact inaccessible to you—meaning that if it were before you

26

in your present condition, you could not make anything of it. However, if you are of slightly higher than moderate intelligence, and are willing to devote a rather large amount of time and effort to the study of mathematics and physics, you can be put in a position to understand the evidence and judge for yourself. That is: you can become a physicist. To say that the evidence for the pi-meson is publicly verifiable does not mean that it is easy to comprehend, that it is available right now to the general public; it only means that someone who follows a stated procedure can arrive at comprehension."

The mystic's argument is parallel: "You refuse to believe anything not 'publicly verifiable,' as you put it? Very well. You say that physics is publicly verifiable, though admitting that to understand physics one must become a physicist. Surely then it cannot be unreasonable for us mystics to tell you that the way to understand mysticism is to become a mystic. Now here is the way you do it: fifteen minutes of contemplation the first day, increasing fifteen minutes a day for six weeks; the following breathing exercises . . . ; fasting . . . ; mortifications, etc., etc. After this, your chance of being illuminated will be a fair one. . . . Too difficult? Why should it be easier to penetrate the secret of the universe than to understand the pi-meson? You ask whether we guarantee success if the regimen is followed? Of course we don't! But then, what physicist ever guaranteed that everybody could become a physicist?"

The analogy is plausible. But there are disanalogies:

Item: Physicists, if they cannot talk to laymen, can still talk to one another without difficulty. But there is no technical vocabulary of mysticism enabling mystics to converse about their experiences in a precise manner even among themselves.

Item: There is an agreed curriculum for the study of

physics. There is no agreed road to mystical illumination. The manuals vary in their prescriptions, and whole sects of mystics reject set procedures altogether.

Item: The discipline required of the would-be physicist is entirely intellectual. At no point in the proceedings is it made a condition of progress that he "have faith," reform his morals, or anything of that sort. It is otherwise with the mystic path.

Here we have a very serious objection. To lay it down that one must "believe in order to understand" is nothing less than to refuse to play the rational game. So-called evidence that counts as evidence only to believers is just not evidence at all in any recognizable sense of the word. It would be hardly less objectionable to claim that the evidence can be vouchsafed only to the "pure"—and practically it would amount to the same thing, since religions tend to make belief an indispensable condition of "purity." In plain language, what is being said is just this: "Unless you can manage somehow to believe without evidence, you cannot get any evidence." "Unless you really believe in fairies, you will never see any."

Only two considerations prevent this last objection from being fatal to the mystics' claim to rationality. The first is that we probably malign the mystics in complaining that they *always* make faith an antecedent condition of illumination. Perhaps there have been cases of unbelievers being converted all at once by an unsought-for and unexpected ecstasy: St. Paul on the road to Damascus (though that was a vision rather than a rapture). If not, even so the mystic might say that it *could* happen were it not for the lamentable fact that unbelievers, because of their unbelief, are unwilling to tread the rocky path. (Unbelievers in pi-mesons seldom bother to learn physics.) Second, it is after all conceivable that there should really be fairies, who are, however, too shy, or uninterested in proselytizing, to display themselves to vulgar cavilers; similarly, it is conceivable that the believer, and only the believer, is favored by evidence that would convert an unbeliever if it were presented to him—but there is a "law of supernature" that such pearls are not to be cast before swine. We may say if we like that such additional saving hypotheses become somewhat strained, besides being repugnant to our sense of what is fair in the rational game.

It seems fair to conclude, however, that while "But you can become a mystic" may have some force against the flat denial of evidential value to mystical experience, the question is not to be settled this way. For the rejoinder is not enough like "But you can become a physicist" and too much like "But you can become a telepathist." It behooves us all the more, therefore, to appraise the contention that mystical experience is not really different, in those respects that bear on its adequacy as evidence, from ordinary experience; and that, in consequence, people who do not have it ought to listen to people who do have it, for the same excellent reason that the blind should pay attention to the sighted.

Mystics often argue that the privacy and incommunicability of their experiences are characteristics shared by all experiences; the only reason they are noticed in the case of mysticism, but unnoticed about drunkenness, is that mysticism is rarer than drunkenness. But it is absurd to make mere rarity into an incurable evidential defect.

Some philosophers say that every experience is private and incommunicable. What is meant by this paradox is that the quality of the experience—"how it feels," roughly speaking —cannot be put into language. We can communicate its form

—how long it takes, what brings it on, how it affects one's blood pressure, etc.; and we can say what it feels *like*. That is all.

When we describe what an experience is like, we do so via assumptions about antecedent experiences of our hearers and about their qualitative similarity to ours.

A: "What does the pudding taste like?" B: "It must have bananas in it." Such an interchange is as successful as any communication could be. If A has not been told all about the pudding, he knows something anyway; he can anticipate the taste of it, and when he tastes it he will not be surprised; he can use the information to decide whether he wants to order a portion for himself; and so on.

The communication is successful only because B can assume that A already knows how a banana tastes. Such an assumption is a reasonable one to make of an adult twentieth-century English-speaking person. Bananas are discriminable physical objects. I bite one; a certain taste-experience ensues. This experience I name "banana-taste." I see someone else bite a banana; I assume that some experience then occurs in him. By the rules of language this experience, whatever its quality, its feel, will be named "banana-taste" likewise. I assume furthermore that the quality of his experience is similar to mine.

A philosopher might challenge this assumption: "How do you know that his banana-taste isn't like your carrot-taste, or even quite unlike any experience you have ever had? All you know, and all you can know, is that he has taken a bite from the banana. What happens then is private to him; there is no conceivable way for you to find out what the quality of his experience is. You mustn't be deceived by the identity of name into supposing you know it in its innerness."

One could meet this challenge by pointing to the publicly

observable similarity of his banana to my banana, the similarity of this physiology to mine, and the principle "same cause same effect." If the philosopher is not satisfied by this reasoning, the only thing to do is to say to him: "It doesn't matter. He has some sort of experience when he bites a banana. Whatever its quality, that quality is repeated, so he tells us, whenever he bites any banana. Now, when I tell him the pudding tastes as if it has banana mashed up in it, I succeed in conveying the only kind of information that could be called for in the circumstances: I give him a basis for expecting that repeatable quality (whatever its innerness may be) to be repeated yet once more if he tastes the pudding."

We have touched here on a point of some importance: success in communicating does not depend on knowledge shared by the communicators of the respective feels of their experiences. As far as language is concerned, the banana-taste simply is the experience one has when one bites a banana. To be sure, I believe, I think reasonably, that the quality or content of your banana-taste experience is like mine. But if this were not true—indeed, even if I knew that it was not true—I should go on talking about bananas in just the same way. We can sum this up by saying that language conveys the structure of experience but not its content.

Let us illustrate further. If someone reports that bananas taste just like oranges to him, then we know that his experience is *not* like ours; but what we know in this case is that the structures of our experiences differ: he fails to make a discrimination that we make. This is how we tell that some persons are color-blind. But as long as his discriminations correlate with differences in the stimuli in the same way that ours do, there is no way we can tell whether the private experiential basis of his discriminations—the qualities, feels, contents of his experiences—are like ours or not.

Nor does language even attempt to describe contents as distinguished from structures, as is indicated by the clumsy and artificial vocabulary we have just had to employ in trying to talk about this distinction. If we suppose that it does, that is because we make a same-structure-same-contents assumption. (I am not questioning that assumption, only pointing it out.)

Another way of making this point is by analyzing what happens when one is asked to describe an experience to someone who has never had it. The same banana will do, if we suppose we lived a hundred years earlier, when bananas were uncommon in the northern hemisphere. You have never tasted a banana. I have. You ask me to describe its taste to you. All I can do is say that it tastes more like *this* than like *that* (where *this* and *that* are things you have tasted), though not *quite* the same as *this*. If I am clever enough, it may occur to me (as it did to one Victorian) to describe it as "a sort of pineapple-flavoured marrow."

The more disparate the experience I try to describe is from any my hearer has gone through, the greater the difficulties. "What does straight whisky taste like?" "Well, it is aromatic, and bitter-sweet—more sweet than bitter—and it burns on the way down." "Like very hot sweetened coffee, then?" "No, no, not that kind of bitter-sweet, and certainly not that kind of burn."

The climax is reached when one struggles to describe the experiences of one sense modality to a person deprived of that sense: "To describe colors to a blind man." One can say something meaningful and suggestive even here: somehow scarlet really is more like a trumpet blast than aquamarine is, and busy wallpaper is rather like walking over gravel; but this is not much help. If it is any help at all, that is because there is some remote similarity between seeing a tomato and hearing a trumpet. Even so, only the person with sight can know this; the blind man must take it on faith.

To return now to the mystic and his defense: the ineffability of mystic ecstasy is just this same ineffability of content that is met in every experience, no matter how commonplace. When the mystic speaks to the nonmystic haltingly, in puzzling metaphors, the same sort of thing is occurring as when a man with sight tries to describe vision to a blind man. The only difference is that mystic experience, not being sensory at all, lacks even that tenuous analogy to our other senses that sight has to hearing.

All that is very well, the nonmystic replies; but those who can see have a rich and precise vocabulary in which they can communicate with one another about their visual experiences; whereas, we must repeat, there is no analogous vocabulary shared by the mystics with which they can communicate among themselves. They talk to one another in the same puzzling metaphors that they address to the general public.

It is not too difficult for the mystic to counter this objection. The reason there is a rich vocabulary of visual terms is that visual experience is structurally complex: there are all sorts of different things to see, and all of them have names. The same is true, though in less degree, of other sense modalities. Mystic ecstasy, on the other hand, is absolutely simple structurally: there is just one object (if it is permissible to use this word) of the experience. Suppose there were just one visible object: say, the sun. Then men of vision would have very little to say to each other: "Have you seen *it* today?" would be about the extent of this talk. They would probably not even have such a word as "bright," since there would be nothing dim to contrast it with; only the total darkness of everything else, wholly other than the sun. Perhaps they would attempt to convey their experience to the blind by saying that the sun is "loud": it comes closer to the mark to describe the sun as loud than as soft, though of course one should not suppose that it has the same kind of loudness that a thunderclap has. (The burn of whisky is not the same kind of burn as that of hot coffee.) But all these difficulties notwithstanding, they really would be seeing the sun, which really would be "out there"; moreover, they could explain why noonday is warmer than midnight, etc.

This analogy goes a long way toward vindicating mysticism against the ineffability objection. Let us see how far it can be stretched.

Our supposition must be that the sun is the only thing visible and that very few persons are able to see at all. Our question is: Would it be reasonable for the sightless majority to believe in the existence of the sun on the basis of what the few visionaries told them? Our supposition does not answer the question of itself; a belief can be true without being reasonable.

The question of reasonableness, here as always, turns on the question of what kind of evidence in support of the assertion could be produced by the sighted to the blind. We have already suggested that the sighted could explain why noonday is warmer than midnight. Let us follow this out.

The blind people are already aware of two warmth cycles, one of twenty-four hours, the other of 365 days. These cycles are for them brute facts; the visionaries explain them by the movements of the sun, the "source" of warmth. The blind people know that tomatoes will not grow inside wooden structures, but will grow outdoors or in glass houses. The men with sight explain that this is because wood obscures ("stops the sound of"?) the sun, whereas glass does not. The blind men, by endless fiddling with a convex lens, occasionally succeed in setting tinder on fire; the men with sight accomplish this every time straight off.

Now in such circumstances it would be reasonable for the blind men to believe the seers, precisely because the blind men would already have inferred the existence and properties of the sun! The seer would explain the daily cycle of warmth by saying: "There is a big fire up above that moves from east to west." But the blind men, familiar with the warming properties of terrestrial fire, would already have suspected the existence of a moving fiery object, and would have confirmed their hypothesis by various methods: the simplest to describe would perhaps be a convex lens, the position of which was governed by a heat-sensitive servomechanism. Blind men could learn for themselves, simply by feeling, the differential properties of wood and glass with respect to passage of the sun's rays. These men would therefore conclude, correctly, that the seers possessed the ability to perceive directly what "ordinary men" could know only indirectly, via apparatus and associated theory—as if someone were to arise among us who could "hear" radio waves, or "see" electrons making quantum jumps.

It is not to the point to object that our suppositious case is fantastic, that a race of blind men could not stay alive, much less contrive heat-sensitive servomechanisms. We have been talking about what is possible in principle; and it should be fairly easy to see that a blind man could know all of physics —not in the trivial sense of taking on credit what men with sight told him, but by having conducted the fundamental experiments and made the inferences from them. As far as knowing the structure of the physical world is concerned— and that is what physics is solely concerned with—sight is in principle a dispensable sense.

These assertions may be unconvincing, however, and justifying them would take us too far afield. Well then, let us suppose, if you prefer, a more plausible race of blind men—men incapable of building any sort of physicists' apparatus, quite unacquainted with technology. And suppose, now, that the seers appear. Then the brute fact of the warmth cycles is "explained" by the existence and travels of the sun. Really, however, this would be no explanation at all; one brute fact known to the blind would be correlated with another brute fact known to the seer. There would be no reason for the blind man to believe in the seer's fact, first, because there would be no way for him to check up on it; second, because there would be no way of connecting the two facts. Cf. someone who purported to "explain" baldness by a nonsensuous emanation from the bald man's pate.

We can now conclude this excursion into the land of the blind. If seers arose among the blind, the blind would have reason to believe what the seers told them only insofar as the seers' assertions were amenable to checking procedures that could be carried out by the blind men themselves, or at least were of the same general nature as checkable assertions. The qualification is necessary because, for example, it would be reasonable for the blind to believe seers' descriptions of sunspots, even if the blind had no independent means of verifying their existence—if the seers had first established their credibility by making a sufficient number of checkable statements. The main point is that it would not be reasonable for the blind to believe in the sun solely on the testimony of the seers. And we must not be misled by the fact that what the seers reported would be true.

If we now apply this analogy to the case of the mystic in relation to the nonmystic, it is easy to see what conclusion we must come to. At best, it is reasonable for the nonmystic to believe the mystic only if the mystic makes some checkable statements that show him to have a power of directly experiencing what the nonmystic knows about only indirectly—but nonetheless knows about independently of the mystic. In other words, the mystic, just like the seer of visions, could confirm and to some degree extend the nonmystic's knowledge of God—but his testimony could not be sufficient in itself to establish that knowledge in the first instance on a rational basis.

Mystics might object to the application of this analogy, on the ground that the blind-man-and-seer case refers only to what can be reasonably believed about facts in the realm of nature, whereas the mystic claims access to facts (if that is not a misleading word) about supernature. The mystic will tell us that he does not claim a "sixth sense" or anything like a sense; hence conclusions about the circumstances in which we should credit someone with having an extra sense are simply irrelevant.

Actually, however, we have given the mystic more than a run for his money. It must be harder to establish the possession of a faculty of intuition totally unlike a sense, for seeing into a realm totally unlike nature, than to present reasons for believing that one has some mode like the ordinary five senses of apprehending facts in some ways like those of ordinary experience.

Summary and Conclusions

IT is reasonable to believe that Gustavus VI is the present King of Sweden because the teacher says so. It is reasonable to believe that there are platypuses because we have seen them in the zoo. In Part I we have considered whether in the same or analogous senses it is reasonable to believe that there is a god. Our conclusion is negative.

It might be reasonable to believe the assertion of an authority simply because he was of such character that there was a rational compulsion to give credence to whatever he said. In order for any being to be regarded as a self-justifying authority, however, he would have to exhibit at least the superhuman, miraculous powers of a nature-controller, i.e., *be* a deity of some sort. In the most favorable case he could only give us reason to believe that he was a god, not God. But it would be extremely difficult, if not impossible, for the observer confronted with such a being to know that he was witnessing an exhibition of nature-control rather than experiencing a hallucination. And for someone not a witness to know or have reason to believe it probable that such an exhibition had occurred would be impossible altogether, because of the fallibility of testimony. Consequently, it is doubtful whether any human being has ever had, on the basis of observation of miracles, any reason to believe that there is a god; and it is certain that no one has ever had any such reason on account of what he was told by others.

Nor can a rational ground for theistic belief be founded on experiences of any other sort. Visions and voices differ from the case just considered only in their privacy, and this is sufficient to dismiss them as even less authoritative. On the other hand, mystical experience—experience quite unlike everyday perception or feeling—is more difficult to evaluate. For this reason—and also because of my uneasiness at pontificating concerning an experience I have never had—I am not so sure of the conclusions reached on this subject. At any rate, I would not quarrel with James when he says that "mystical states, when well developed, usually are, and have the right to be, absolutely authoritative over the individuals to whom they come."[6] (But compare: "States of delirium tremens, when well developed, usually are, and have the right to be, absolutely authoritative. . . ." We found no compelling reason for refusing to assimilate mystical states to delirium tremens.) Surely no one can disagree with his further conclusion: "No authority emanates from [mystical states] which should make it a duty for those who stand outside of them to accept their revelations uncritically"[7]—nor indeed to accept them at all.

Once more let it be emphasized that authority and religious experience are not here condemned as incapable of having any bearing on the question of the existence of a god, or of God. The rejection is of more modest scope. In the first place, we have delineated certain conceivable circumstances in which authority or experience might tend to establish such existence;

[6] James, *op. cit.*, Lect. XVII, p. 422.
[7] *Ibid.*

as to these, the claim is only that no one now has reason to believe that the conditions have ever been fulfilled. Second, we have left open the possibility that further psychological investigation might establish that mystical ecstasy is not at all to be assimilated to delusory states. In that case, much more credence should be given to the claim that they "have the right to be absolutely authoritative over the individuals to whom they come"; and if so, it might even be "a duty for those who stand outside of them to accept their revelations"—though not "uncritically." Third, let me point out just once more that if the arguments of Part I are sound, they show only that authority and immediate experience cannot stand alone—they cannot of themselves, in the absence of any other reason, establish the existence of a god. In the following parts we shall take up the search for independent grounds; if they are found, then authority and experience become valuable as possibly corroborative evidence. Last, the senses of "reason" in Part I are strictly those illustrated at the beginning of the part and in this summary; we leave open for investigation in Parts IV and V the possibility that there is some other defensible sense of the word according to which authority and religious experience do afford reasons for believing that there is a god.

Part II

THE TRADITIONAL ARGUMENTS

IN concluding that experience by itself cannot provide a reason for believing that there is a god, we have by no means exhausted the possibilities of there being a rational basis for theism, in some ordinary sense of "reason." There remain two such senses to consider:

The first is the sense in which we say we have reason to believe that there exist two integer roots of the equation $x^2 - 4 = 0$ (*viz.*, 2 and -2). Here we see the truth of this, not by perceiving the roots sitting "out there"; nor is our knowledge based in any degree on our experience of the world. Rather, we say this truth "follows from" or "is contained in" the very ideas involved, which are such that these roots must exist, could not possibly not exist. It is pure reason, unaided (or uncontaminated) by experience of the senses, that tells us this.

It seems fitting that our knowledge of God should be of the same pure sort. In the celebrated ontological argument of St. Anselm, the attempt has been made to demonstrate the existence of God in this way, without any appeal at all to mere empirical facts, to what happens to be the case as opposed to what must be so.

Both of the other traditional proofs purport to show that the existence of God may be inferred with certainty or high probability from the facts given in perception. The cosmological argument is: something exists; and if anything exists, God must exist as its cause or reason. The argument from design infers God as the source of order in the world, as the reason why the universe is not utterly chaotic.

Despite the onslaughts of skeptics, these two arguments continue to show great vitality. According to a survey made by the author, rather more than half the college students to whom the arguments were briefly presented regarded them as convincing.

The Ontological Argument

DISCUSSIONS of the traditional arguments for the existence of God usually begin with an account of the ontological argument (argument from the concept of being), as formulated by St. Anselm of Canterbury (1033–1109). The gist of it is this:

"God" means "the perfect Being." "Perfect Being" means "Being combining perfect power, perfect goodness, etc., *and perfect reality*." Hence to say "God does not exist" amounts to uttering the contradiction "The Being which is (among other attributes) perfectly real is not real." Therefore the statement "God exists" is necessarily true. Indeed, it is inconceivable that God should not exist, as it is inconceivable that there should be a round square or that there should not be a prime number greater than 29, though one might (mistakenly) think that he conceives it, entertains the possibility.

This argument has had a perennial fascination for philosophers. Some of the greatest, including Descartes and Leibniz, have defended it. At one time, even Bertrand Russell thought it valid:

The Traditional Arguments

I remember the precise moment, one day in 1894, as I was walking along Trinity Lane, when I saw in a flash (or thought I saw) that the ontological argument is valid. I had gone out to buy a tin of tobacco; on my way back, I suddenly threw it up in the air, and exclaimed as I caught it: "Great Scott, the ontological argument is sound."[8]

Philosophers—especially those, like the three just named, who are also mathematicians—are intrigued by the argument because it purports to bridge the gap between the realms of mathematical and factual truths. If it is valid, then there is at least one truth of fact, one true statement about what exists "out there," that is demonstrable by procedures like those used in mathematical reasoning, and that shares, moreover, in the absolute certainty (inconceivability of the opposite) that attaches to the theorems of logic and mathematics. Pure reason in an armchair can then tell us something—something of the last importance—about what there is. Mathematical statements do not have this character; though it is certain that two apples and two more apples make four apples, one cannot infer from this alone that there are any apples: cf. "two unicorns and two more unicorns make four unicorns."

One might suppose that theologians would be equally enthusiastic. For this argument, alone among the traditional three, is such that if it proves anything at all, it patently proves just what theologians are concerned to prove: the existence of God, the perfect Being, the Being than which a greater cannot be conceived—not perhaps merely a big bang or a limited universe-artificer. Yet very few theologians have espoused the argument. On its first appearance it was severely

[8] Bertrand Russell, "My Mental Development," in *The Philosophy of Bertrand Russell*, Paul A. Schilpp, ed. (Evanston, Ill.: Library of Living Philosophers, Inc., 1944), p. 10.

criticized by the monk Gaunilo, who pointed out that *something* must be wrong with it, for if not, then by similar reasoning one ought to be able to define into existence a perfect island. Subsequently, St. Thomas Aquinas rejected it; and thus the matter has stood to this day. Perhaps this bespeaks the greater skepticism of theologians as compared with philosophers.

St. Anselm's Formulation of the Argument

Anselm's writings are among the most charming to be found on the theological shelf. Particularly attractive is the passage in the *Proslogium* in which the ontological argument is set out. It is in the form of a commentary on the words of the Psalmist, "The fool hath said in his heart, There is no god." Anselm sets out to show that such a one in very truth is a fool, since what he utters is a contradiction.

In the following presentation, I preserve Anselm's words as far as possible, only abridging and altering the order slightly. (GCB = Being than which a greater cannot be conceived.)

1. Whatever is understood exists in the understanding.

2. When the fool hears of the GCB, he understands what he hears.

3. Therefore something exists in the understanding, at least, than which nothing greater can be conceived.

4. Suppose the GCB exists in the understanding alone: then it can be conceived to exist in reality;

5. which is greater.

6. Therefore if that than which nothing greater can be conceived exists in the understanding alone, the very Being than which nothing greater can be conceived is one than which a greater can be conceived.

7. Obviously this is impossible.

8. Assuredly that than which nothing greater can be conceived cannot exist in the understanding alone.

9. There is no doubt that there exists a Being than which nothing greater can be conceived, and it exists both in the understanding and in reality. (This is God.)

Criticism of the Argument

There are many ways of showing what is wrong with this reasoning. The most famous is Kant's doctrine that existence is not a predicate. When we say, "God is good," we predicate goodness of God, that is, we assert that God has the property of being good. Anselm assumes that in a similar way, when we say, "God is real," we ascribe a property, reality, to God. However (Kant objects), reality adds nothing to our conception of anything: "A hundred imaginary thalers have all the predicates of a hundred real thalers." If they did not, we should never be able to compare our conception with the object, to see whether our conception was *realized*. Before Kant, Hume had made the same point:

To reflect on any thing simply, and to reflect on it as existent, are nothing different from each other. That idea, when conjoin'd with the idea of any object, makes no addition to it. Whatever we conceive, we conceive to be existent. Any idea we please to form is the idea of a being; and the idea of a being is any idea we please to form.[9]

This refutation, however, is not definitive principally because the question "Is x a property?" has a precise and unambiguous answer only in the context of an ideal (completely formalized) language; and neither English, nor German, nor medieval Latin is such an ideal language. It is always open to

[9] David Hume, *A Treatise of Human Nature* (1739), Bk. I, Pt. II, sec. 6.

a partisan of Anselm to reply: "Existence *is* a property—though admittedly of a unique kind; but every property is unique in some respect."

I shall try to criticize the argument in the spirit of Kant without invoking this somewhat dubious and controversial doctrine as self-evident. I shall take each premise of the argument, translate it into a synonymous expression not containing the word "exists," and see what happens then.

A minimum of apparatus must first be developed: the distinction between use and mention of a word, and the concept of denoting.

Suppose we overhear someone saying: "Schmidt understands horses," and we hear no more of the conversation. Then we cannot tell whether the speaker meant (*a*) Schmidt is knowledgeable about horses: easily senses their moods, knows what pleases them and what makes them nervous, can tell the skittish ones at a glance, and so on; or (*b*) Schmidt is making progress in English; he has just learned that the English for "Pferde" is "horses."

Context normally settles easily in which sense the sentence is to be taken. If it is *written* correctly, the ambiguity cannot arise in the first place, for sense (*b*) requires quotation marks around "horses." These marks serve to indicate that it is the *word* "horses" that is being talked about, not the animals to which the word refers. The word "horses" is being *mentioned* (talked about or written about), not *used* (to refer to non-linguistic entities).

It is important to note that although in "Schmidt understands horses," the word "horses" is used to refer to animals that exist in the real world, a word can be used even when there is no actual object named by the word: e.g., "Unicorns are rare" contains a use-occurrence of "unicorns."

Suppose, now, that we utter the true sentence: "Unicorns

don't exist." Since it is clearly not the *word* "unicorn" the existence of which we are denying, we must class this occurrence of the word as a use. This leads us to the question: What *is* the use of "unicorn" in this sentence? Some philosophers have supposed that the only kind of use a word has (at any rate, the only kind of use a noun has) is to refer; hence, since "unicorn" is not a meaningless noise, and is successfully used in the sentence, there must be some sort of thing—an idea, a Subsistent Entity—that is the referent.

Such metaphysics, however, can be avoided. First, the somewhat misleading term "use" should be nontendentiously defined as "successful linguistic employment other than mention." Second, we note that the meaning we convey in the sentence "Unicorns don't exist" can be just as well expressed by saying, "The word 'unicorn' doesn't denote anything." Here "denote" has this sense: " 'W' denotes W's" means "The word 'W' is the name of objects of the W-kind." Then "W's don't exist," "W's aren't real," "There aren't any W's" are all expressions that come to the same as " 'W' doesn't denote anything." Here we have erected a kind of bridge between use and mention: sentences asserting (or denying) existence, in which the word designating what is said (or denied) to exist is used, can be exactly rephrased as sentences asserting (or denying) that the same word, but now mentioned, has a denotation.

We can now return to the argument.

The first three premises constitute a subargument to show that the GCB "exists in the understanding." We can concede this, with the proviso that "exists in the understanding" means no more than "is understood." If anyone objects to this, it is incumbent on him to formulate a set of circumstances in which it could be truly said that some *x* existed in the understanding without being understood by anyone; or else, someone understood x, but x did not exist in the understanding.

The occurrences of "GCB" in the second and third premises are mentions. What the fool understands "when he hears of the GCB" is the *phrase;* it is clear at any rate that this is all that Anselm claims.

We can then paraphrase these premises as follows:

1'. Whatever is understood is understood.
2'. Someone understands "GCB."
3'. Therefore someone understands "GCB."

True, the paraphrase is trivial. But that is no serious objection, either to Anselm or to the translation. Anselm's purpose in these sentences was to elucidate his meaning of "exist in the understanding"; ours is better served by emphasizing the identity in meaning of this phrase with "be understood"; we accomplish this by reducing both terms to the same one.

The second premise, which is the same as the conclusion, is a factual statement to the effect that somebody (nearly everybody) understands the meaning of the phrase "Being than which a greater cannot be conceived." Some critics have objected that this premise is false, since the Being in question = God, and nobody understands (has adequate knowledge of) God. But this complaint seems to miss the point. We must grant that no one understands God, if to understand Him means to understand His motives, have His wisdom, etc. In this sense I do not understand the President of France, nor do I understand the phrase "richest man in the world" in the sense of knowing what it would feel like to be in that position. I certainly understand the words though, in the sense of knowing what the criteria are for identifying the occupants of these positions. Now it seems sufficient for Anselm's argument that the fool should understand "GCB" in this less grandiose sense: that the GCB should be the wisest, most powerful, best, etc., Being imaginable; and certainly one can understand what is intended by a phrase like "wisest possible" without being oneself as wise as possible. In fact, our own requirement is more stringent than is necessary. All that is needed for the argument is the concession that "GCB" should not be meaningless; and this condition may be met, even if one cannot specify criteria for applying the term to an object. "Most beautiful statue ever carved" is a meaningful phrase, though I do not know how to go about identifying its referent.

We come now to the meatier premises. The fourth consists of two clauses, the first being "Suppose the GCB exists in the understanding alone." In accordance with our rule for translating such expressions, the part of this not containing the word "alone" should be rendered "Suppose 'GCB' is understood," while the force of "alone" is to deny that the GCB "exists in reality." And since this comes to asserting that " 'GCB' does not denote anything," the whole "Suppose . . ." clause becomes: "Suppose 'GCB' is understood, but 'GCB' does not denote anything."

The second clause is "then it [the GCB] can be conceived to exist in reality." This is translated as "then 'GCB' can be conceived to denote something"; and the translation of the entire premise is:

4'. Suppose "GCB" is understood, but "GCB" does not denote anything: then "GCB" can be conceived to denote something;

This is the point at which Hume and Kant attack the argument, on the ground that there is no difference between conceiving and conceiving to denote; since, moreover, conceiving does not appear to differ from understanding, at least in the context of this argument, the premise reduces to the triviality:

4″. Suppose "GCB" is understood, but "GCB" does not denote anything: then "GCB" can be understood;
and the argument collapses.

Anselm, however, clearly believed that there was a difference between conceiving merely, and conceiving to denote; and this is a prima facie reason to think there is some difference. But if we ask ourselves what the difference could be, we must conclude that it is one in attitude toward a conception, not in the conception itself; and this is to concede the Kant-Hume objection. Although just idly thinking about mermaids is not the same as believing that there are mermaids, the difference does not lie in the conception. "Mermaid" means "half-woman half-fish" for believer and unbeliever alike; the image conjured up when the word is pronounced is the same; the difference is that the believer believes this image to correspond to something of flesh and blood, whereas the unbeliever does not.

In any event, the argument can hardly survive scrutiny of its next premise:

5. which is greater.

The "which" refers to "existing in reality" (*sc.* the GCB), so that our paraphrase must be:

5′. "GCB" denoting something is greater than "GCB" not denoting anything.

The trouble with this rendering is that it does not appear to have any intelligible meaning. If the rephrasing is at fault, then there must be something wrong with our previous analysis of the equivalence between "X exists" and " 'X' denotes something." That may be; it is up to the objector to investigate the possibility.

Anselm's meaning is perhaps something like this: thinking of mermaids is different from not thinking at all; ergo, when one hears of mermaids, and understands what one hears, one is conceiving of *something:* to wit, something imaginary. But imaginary mermaids are poor thin things—just barely objects— as compared with (say) hippopotamuses of flesh and blood. Similarly, when one hears of the Greatest Conceivable Being, and understands what one hears, one is conceiving *something* —at worst, something imaginary, just barely an object. But it would be ludicrous to suppose that such a wraith could really be the Greatest Conceivable Being:

6. Therefore if that than which nothing greater can be conceived exists in the understanding alone, the very being than which nothing greater can be conceived is one than which a greater can be conceived.

7. Obviously this is impossible.

The if clause of premise 6 is easily put as "if 'GCB' is understood but does not denote anything"; but the remainder defies this treatment. At first sight it looks as if it should be rendered, "then the GCB is not the GCB" (in which "GCB," for the first time in the argument, is *used*). If so, however, the whole premise would be a glaring non sequitur, and besides, the then clause and premise 7 would beg the question; for it is only "obviously impossible" for an *existent thing* not to be identical with itself. Let us suppose, then, that the two occurrences of "GCB" in the then clause are mentions: "then 'GCB' is not identical with 'GCB.'" This is an improvement, as it does not beg the question; but it is still a non sequitur. A concept cannot be self-contradictory just because it denotes nothing. Reality does not come in different grades, qualities, or concentrations.

Even if we grant Anselm his fundamental assumption of grades of reality, his argument is still invalid. Let us assume for the sake of argument that there are two species of existence, a higher and a lower, and that by the very nature of the concept, "GCB" must partake of the higher. We grant even that it is part of the concept that GCB must exist in reality, not merely in the understanding. It still does not follow that there exists in reality the Greatest Conceivable Being. All that can be concluded is that *if* there is a GCB, it must be real—a trivial and harmless inference.

We show this in the following way. The ontological argument can be abbreviated thus:

1. "GCB" means, among other things, "perfectly Real Being."
2. Therefore the following statement is self-contradictory: "The GCB is not real."
3. Therefore the GCB *is* real.

Consider now the parallel argument:

1. "Myriagon" means "10,000-sided plane figure."
2. Therefore the following statement is self-contradictory: "The myriagon does not have 10,000 sides."
3. Therefore there is a myriagon with 10,000 sides.

This latter argument is easily seen to be fallacious. All that follows from the premises is that *if* anything is a myriagon, then necessarily it has 10,000 sides, neither more nor less. In exactly the same way, all that follows from the premises of the ontological argument is that *if* anything is the GCB, then necessarily that thing is real. There is no way of getting rid of the *if* by logic alone. If we grant that "unreal GCB" is a contradiction in terms, all we can infer is the Irish conclusion that "if it's unreal it can't be the GCB."

Consequence of the Failure of the Ontological Argument

If this short refutation (which is also to be found in Kant) is sufficient to dispose of the matter, then was not the long discussion of the existence-is-not-a-predicate business superfluous? No, because one point of great importance can be derived from the latter but not from the former: "logically necessary being" is a phrase without meaning. The shorter refutation suffices to show that the concept cannot guarantee the existence of its own referent; but it leaves open the possibility that God's essence entails His existence in the logical sense of entailment. In that case, the statement "God exists" would have not merely factual but logical certainty. If, however, denotation can, as a matter of logic, never be contained in a concept, then nothing—not even God—can have existence logically guaranteed it. There is not then, nor can there be, anything the nonexistence of which is inconceivable or involves contradiction.

Most philosophers have gone further and concluded that no meaning can be assigned to the phrase "necessary existence." They have then argued that the cosmological argument, which purposes to show that God necessarily exists, must in consequence be invalid; in other words (following Kant), the cosmological argument rests on the ontological and falls with it. As I shall point out in discussing the cosmological argument, however, it does not seem to me that one is obliged to interpret "God is the necessary Being" as meaning the same as "The sentence 'God exists' is necessarily true." "Necessary being" can mean, and I think does mean in most theological contexts, Being not subject to limitation by any other Being; unconditioned Being.

The Cosmological Argument

ALL versions of the cosmological argument have this general form: the universe, regarded as a whole, cannot be self-sufficient; for it to exist there must be, outside it and prior to it, some real Being of such a kind as to constitute the reason for the existence of the universe; such a Being must be God.

While the cosmological argument contains a factual premise, to wit, *something exists*, it contains only this non-controversial reference to matter of fact. All the rest of the edifice is constructed of and by pure reason. If, as we have suggested, it is particularly appropriate that God's existence should be demonstrable by the intellect unaided by the senses, it would be overly nice to complain that this argument does not completely fulfill that requirement.

There *is* something—at the very least, as St. Augustine and Descartes pointed out, there is indubitably the intellect of the reasoner. But why should there be something rather than nothing? The argument regards this as a legitimate question, to which the only ultimately satisfactory answer is: Because of God.

There are two main forms of the argument, accordingly as

the relation of God to the universe is conceived to be that of a first cause in time—God as instigator of the first event; or that of reason for nature—God as reason to which we should inevitably be led, whether or not the cosmos had a beginning in time. I shall call these the crude and subtle cosmological arguments, respectively.

First Cause Argument

This argument is implied in the common rhetorical question "If there is no God, then who or what made the world?" Put explicitly, it is as follows:

1. Everything has a cause. For everything that exists (E), there is some other thing (C), which existed before E came into existence; and C produced E—that is, without C there would have been no E. C itself was produced by a pre-existing C', and so on.

2. But not ad infinitum: the series of causes and effects must have a beginning.

3. The first cause must have been a Being capable of producing everything else in the series. For the effect cannot exceed the cause; if it did, that part which exceeded it would be uncaused.

4. Such a Being must be an infinite Being, i.e., God.

Refutation of the First Cause Argument

Every premise of this argument is vulnerable. If the universe, however great, is finite, then we cannot legitimately infer an infinite Being as its cause; the argument at most proves a deity, not God. But perhaps not even that: in the absence of further argumentation, we are left with the possibility that the "big bang," supposed by astrophysicists to have occurred eleven billion years ago, was the first cause: a mere event, lacking (for all we know) personality and intelligence. Furthermore, the notion of "cause" assumed in the argument is somewhat dubious.

All these defects are remediable; but we shall postpone discussion of the remedies until we come to the subtle cosmological argument and the argument from design. For the second premise of the present argument is incurable.

This second premise is to be interpreted, not as asserting that as a matter of fact the universe happens to have had a beginning in time, but that as a matter of logical necessity it must have had one. Now we had best pause a moment to illustrate this distinction, crucial in all forms of the cosmological argument, between matter of fact and matter of logical necessity.

The distinction is illustrated in the following instances:

(1) "If this boulder is pushed over the edge of the precipice, it *must* fall into the gorge"

(2) "If there are two boulders here, and two more over there, then there *must be* four boulders altogether."

In (1) the "must" means "cannot but; there is no physically possible alternative." If asked for the reasons for our expectation, we would reply that that is the way boulders always behave; perhaps we might cite also the universal law of gravitation. We might be tempted to say that it would be inconceivable for the boulder not to fall. But that would be rhetorical exaggeration; we can very easily conceive of what it would be like for the boulder, after being pushed over the brink, to remain suspended in mid-air, to explode, to vanish in a puff of smoke, or to take wing and fly away.

In (2), however, the "must be" means "could not conceivably be more or less than." And here "conceivably" is to be taken literally. One cannot form any conception of what it would be like for a certain collection to contain just two couples, and at the same time, in the same respect, have (say) five members altogether. It is not hard to see why this is so: "2" means "1 + 1," and "4" means "1 + 1 + 1 + 1." Hence "2 + 2 = 4" means "1 + 1 + 1 + 1 = 1 + 1 + 1 + 1" —that is, the ideas symbolized by the marks on the left and right of the "=" are identical. And the rule for the use of the symbol "=" is such that we do not know what it would be like for a quantity not to be equal to itself.[10]

Hence if someone says, "I pushed a boulder over a precipice, and you know what? It just hung there in mid-air!" we will not believe him, though we understand what he is saying. But if he says, "There were two boulders there, and two more, and just those; and do you know what? There were five boulders in all!" we do not know what he means. If he means anything, he must be using the words in some private senses, different from their usual ones.

Now let us get back to the second premise of the first cause argument: "The series of causes and effects must have a beginning." The "must" indicates that logical necessity is being claimed. For if not, all that is claimed is that as a matter of fact the series has a beginning, though it could have been otherwise. In that case, factual evidence for the conclusion would need to be supplied. It is clear, however, that the proponents of the argument have nothing like this in mind. They mean that it is self-evident that the series has a beginning, in the way, say, that it is self-evident that a whole cannot be less than the sum of its parts.

This contention is defensible only if it is logically impossible for a series to have no first member; and the existence of many series, such as the series of all negative integers

$$\ldots, -8, -7, -6, -5, -4, -3, -2, -1$$

[10] This brief illustration is, of course, not offered as a rigorous proof.

shows that there is no such impossibility. When we say that the series of negative integers has no beginning, what we mean is that it is impossible to select a member of the series which has no predecessor; for if it is suggested that some number $-N$ has no predecessor, we can always counter the suggestion by producing the predecessor, namely, $-N-1$.

To be sure, the series of negative integers is an intellectual construction, and the argument concerns things and events "out there" in the world. But to repeat: the argument is not about what happened to exist, but about what *must* have existed. There is nothing logically inconsistent in the notion of a (numerical) series without a first member; therefore there is nothing logically inconsistent in the notion of a series of events, forming a causal chain, and such that at least one event in the chain is associated with each number in the beginningless series.

The attempt has been made to rebut this refutation by arguing in this way: Events are *now* occurring. If there is no beginning to the causal series to which these present events belong, then an infinite series has been already run through. But it is impossible to run through, enumerate successively every member of, an infinite series; therefore the causal series cannot be infinite.

This rejoinder begs the question, since it is only impossible to run through an infinite series in a finite time. Probably what accounts for the plausibility of the argument is the supposition that if the causal series had no beginning, then some event must have occurred infinitely long ago—in the sense that the number of hours between that event and (say) the bombing of Hiroshima is not a finite number, however large. But the conception of an infinite series does not entail that there should be any two given members of that series that are not a finite distance apart in the series; on the contrary, the series of integers is infinite, although the difference between any two given integers is always finite. All that is required for a causal series to be infinite is that however remote two events in the series may be from each other, there are other events remoter still.

Careful thinkers, Christians included, have been aware of these considerations. Those who have held the Judeo-Christian doctrine of a creation of nature out of nothing have followed St. Thomas Aquinas[11] in holding that its truth can be known only by revelation: that as far as the unaided reason can say, the world may or may not have a beginning. Neither view leads to contradiction.

One more observation and we shall be done with this argument. To the common question "If there is no God, then who made the world?" the common retort "Well, who made God?" is a fair one. The first premise of the argument is that everything must have a cause; the conclusion, surprisingly, is its contradictory: some thing, namely God, does *not* have a cause. And those who produce this argument have no ground for objecting to calling God a "thing," for as far as the argument goes, God, the first cause, is just one more member of the totality.

The Subtle Cosmological Argument

The version of the cosmological argument which attempts to show that God must exist as a *reason* for nature, whether nature is finite or infinite in duration, is less well known than the popular version we have just considered. Its essentials were formulated by Plato and Aristotle. Leibniz's version, which our presentation will follow in its main outlines, states it probably as well as it is capable of being put.

[11] St. Thomas Aquinas, *Summa Theologiae,* Pt. I, Ques. XLVI, Art. 2.

A brief preliminary summary of the argument is this: If the world is intelligible, then God exists. But the world is intelligible. Therefore God exists.

"Intelligibility" is defined in terms of the principle of sufficient reason: "There is a Sufficient Reason why everything that is, is so and not otherwise."[12] That is to say, a mere fact, of itself in isolation, is not intelligible, understandable; it becomes intelligible when it is explained—when it is put into a context enabling us to see not just *that* it is, but *why* it is "so and not otherwise."

There are, I am told, at least 93 different kinds of explanation; and though I think that that is an exaggeration, there is admittedly danger in talking, as I am about to do, in terms of only two kinds: mechanical and purposive. These two may be considered, however, as genera embracing many particular species. If they do not jointly exhaust the field, they very nearly do so; and at any rate, it does not seem that anyone has proposed a different kind of explanation that could qualify as universal or cosmic.

A mechanical explanation is one in terms of causes, regularities, laws of nature. It is the type of explanation usually—though as I shall point out in a moment, perhaps not always—encountered in the natural sciences. Explanations of how an airplane works, or why it failed and crashed, are mechanical. Life, or the evolution of a galaxy, is explained mechanically if states at one time are related to states at another via laws, which in the more sophisticated sciences take the form of differential equations; in the less developed disciplines these laws may be no more than statements to the effect that one kind of occurrence has been observed always to be followed by another (cause-effect).

The kind of account we naturally give of why a rational

[12] Leibniz, *Monadology*, sec. 32, and elsewhere.

creature is engaged in a certain activity is purposive or teleological. Such explanations commonly include references to
motives, choices, deliberations, reasons, not to mention emotions and passions.

The contrast between these types of explanation will be in
the focus of our attention throughout this part, and indeed for
the rest of this book. At present it will be sufficient to make
the following points concerning them:

1. Both mechanical and purposive explanations are in everyday use. Why did the lights go out last night? Because there
was a storm upcountry, as a consequence of which a tree was
uprooted and fell across a power line. (Mechanical.) Why
are there so few doors in this house? Because the architect was
an enthusiast for togetherness; moreover his client wanted to
cut expenses as far as possible. (Purposive.)

2. As we see from the examples just given, both types are,
in certain contexts, answers to questions of the form "Why
is . . . ?" It is sometimes said that mechanical explanations are
responses only to "how" questions; but this is not the case.
For the present, we content ourselves with defending the
last statement merely on the ground that the English language
happens to be used this way. To be sure, the "why" in the
question about the lights going out could be replaced by the
locution "How did it come about that . . . ?" But this is
equally true of the question about the doors.

3. Causal and purposive explanations are not always incompatible and are sometimes complementary. Why is Jones
in the prison hospital? (*a*) Because a train hit the car in which
he was riding and dragged it 300 yards. (*b*) Because he
thought to avoid the police by crossing the intersection just in
front of the train. Although either (*a*) or (*b*) might sensibly
be offered as an answer to the question, it may be maintained
that strictly speaking (*b*) presupposes (*a*), or (*a*) is an incom-

plete explanation, or (*a*) and (*b*) are relevant in different contexts. All this may be true. And the more specific we make our question, the more completely determined is the type of explanation that will be appropriate. Where animate agencies are involved, causal and purposive explanations may intertwine. A caused B, because C, wishing D, set E into operation. Moreover, C wished D because F caused him to wish it. Briefly, purposes *are* causes, and are themselves the effects of other causes—sometimes, not always, of other purposes.

4. We note the corollary that it is not obvious which, if either, type of explanation is ultimate. As we have just seen, when we explain some event more and more fully, purposive and causal explanations may oscillate in such a way that there is no clear answer to the question "Yes, but what is the real reason why it happened: cause or purpose?" The question itself is not clear, and may not even have any meaning. In a famous passage in Plato's *Phaedo*,[13] Socrates ridicules the causal (physiological) explanation that might be put forth of his sitting in prison and insists that the true explanation must be in terms of what he and the Athenians "thought best." We may admit that he was right as far as he went; still it would not have been inappropriate to inquire why he and the Athenians thought as they did. The answer to this question might be a causal one, involving economics, climate, gene mutations, or what not.

5. It is not to be taken for granted that scientific explanation is exclusively of the mechanical type. Many scientific advances, especially in the last five centuries, have consisted in producing causal explanations for phenomena previously "explained" in purposive terms: comets, plagues, paranoia, etc. And it is permissible to speculate that eventually science will find it possible to dispense with purposive explanations alto-

[13] Stephanus, ed., pp. 97-99.

gether, in every field of inquiry including the distinctively human. However, if by "scientific" we refer to the actual practices of present-day scientists, we find that certainly psychology and the social sciences have not yet arrived at this point. It still counts as science when one explains that Jones devotes his leisure and his riches to the Society for the Suppression of Vice because he wants to punish himself for his incestuous cravings. (Unconsciously, to be sure—and it is a nice question whether an "unconscious wish" is to be regarded as a cause or a purpose.) In any event, the aim of science is to understand—and science is in no position to determine in advance what the ultimate categories of understanding may turn out to be. For various reasons, it is generally more convenient and fruitful to investigate causes rather than purposes: first, because in some cases there may really be no purpose operating, except possibly very remotely, to produce the phenomenon being investigated, for instance, the appearance of a comet; second, even where a purposive agent (man or animal) is known to be involved, it always operates via causes. But these are dictates of convenience; there is nothing obviously unscientific in the belief that in the last analysis everything happens as it does because God wills it, and that science studies merely the "second causes" whereby He attains His ends.

To return to the principle of sufficient reason: it is just the claim that there are no brute facts, that everything has an explanation—though we may not be able to find out what it is. The principle thus includes the causal principle, that everything has a cause; but it is broader. It says that everything has a cause, or serves a purpose, or both.

But then, why should we accept the principle—if we should? This is a curious question: is there a sufficient reason for accepting the principle of sufficient reason? We shall not face it squarely in this book. It might be maintained that the principle is an assumption that we are obliged to make if our attempts to understand the world are not to be pointless. That is to say, our efforts to explain particular things presuppose that there is some explanation. We do not know what the cause of cancer is, but the biochemist does not for a moment entertain the possibility that cancer has no cause at all. The psychoanalyst does not know what the pattern of his patient's behavior is in all its details; but however "irrational" and apparently meaningless the actions, psychoanalysis is committed to the assumption that there is a meaning to be found in them. Furthermore, the principle does not let us down; our successes in finding reasons why things are "so and not otherwise" are so many confirmations of it, and our failures we ascribe to the difficulty, not the impossibility, of understanding. These may not be adequate reasons for accepting the principle; but we shall simply assume it in what follows.

"So *and not otherwise*." This boulder is here in this gorge; but it "might just as well" have been somewhere else? So it might, considered just in itself. But it used to be on the edge of the precipice above, and someone pushed it; that is why it is here, why it has to be here. But then, why could it not have flown through the air when pushed? Well, heavy bodies, near the surface of the earth, fall when unsupported. This, then, is just a brute fact? No, it follows from the property of matter that bodies attract one another. But why . . . ?

Someone pushed it? He "might just as well" not have pushed it. But inasmuch as unfriendly Indians were pursuing him up the gorge. . . .

Explanation, the finding of sufficient reasons, we see to be a process of ruling out alternative possibilities. Without an explanation we do not know why the boulder should not be in just any old place. The explanation tells us why it is here rather than there—why just this possibility, out of the indefinite or infinite number of conceivable ones, was realized. We know further why it was pushed by just this man at just this time; and so on.

We say that a thing or event is *contingent* if the reason why it is what it is, and not otherwise, is not ascertainable without looking beyond the thing or event itself. To be contingent is just to be dependent on something else, to be the effect of something else. The opposite of "contingent" in this sense is "necessary." Something is necessary if it is what it is no matter what else is the case—if it is something entirely independent, in its existence and all its properties, of the existence and properties of everything else.

We have now defined the term "necessary being." The question is whether there is any reason to believe that a necessary Being exists. (We might as well use capitals, as it will not have escaped the reader that such a Being = God.) The argument proceeds:

It is obvious that there is no necessary Being in nature. This is just another way of saying that everything in nature has a cause. There is no particular thing that would not have been otherwise if something else had been otherwise. Now one may be tempted to say that although this is true of particular things—objects and events—at any rate the laws of nature are exceptions. There might have been more or fewer boulders in this gorge, but the law of gravitation must be what it is. We should note, however, that science explains laws as well as particulars. In Kepler's day, it was one brute fact that heavy bodies near the earth fall when unsupported, another brute fact that smoke goes up, and a third that the planets move around the sun. Newton exhibited the sufficient reason for these in terms of a more comprehensive generalization: given that all matter has the property of gravitating, it follows that all these things must behave as they do and not otherwise. But as to why bodies gravitate, Newton himself knew not, "and [he said] I frame no hypotheses."[14] Before Newton there were the three brute laws we have mentioned, plus a lot of others; after Newton, just one. What are to us, today, the brute laws of gravitation, electromagnetism, nuclear forces, etc., await their explanation in, presumably, a general field theory. Once physicists enunciate such a theory, the number of separate brute facts will be again reduced. But even so, at least one will remain: we shall not know why the general field equation is what it is, and not otherwise. We will be able to imagine other possibilities, and we shall not know why just this one is realized. It will be contingent, but we shall not know on what it is contingent. Or so it appears.

Thus not only is there no necessary thing in nature, but there is no necessary characteristic of nature either. Given that some things in nature are what they are, we understand how it is necessary (relative to them) that other parts of nature are as they are. Given that nature has certain characteristics, we understand why necessarily (relative to them) nature must have certain other characteristics also. But nowhere in nature is there a thing, or a characteristic, of which we can say: This is as it is, and could not be otherwise than it is, no matter what else were to change.

Not only is this last statement true of things in, and characteristics of, nature: nature as a whole is not a necessary Being. The world—the totality of everything that was and is and will be—is only one among an infinitude of possible worlds. By a "possible world" is meant any assemblage of coherently describable things and occurrences. Thus for example one

[14] In note "Concerning the Law of Gravitation," added at close of Book III of *Principia*, 2d ed., 1713.

possible world is that in which everything is exactly the same as in this one, with the single exception that there is a misprint in this line of this book. (More grammatically: it is possible that there should be such a world.) It is possible that your parents might never have met, and in consequence that you would not have existed: we have described another possible world. Still another is inhabited by unicorns, mermaids, and centaurs. This is not to say that such creatures are biologically possible; only that no contradiction is involved in supposing that they could exist were the laws of biology different from what they are. Novelists and painters, including surrealists, describe possible worlds. The only limitation on imagining them—and it is not really a limitation—is that a possible world cannot be such that description of it would involve logical contradiction. Thus there is no possible world containing round squares.

This world that we live in, then, is not the only possible world; but it is the only real or actual world. Now when one state of affairs, out of a plurality of possibilities, is realized, there must be a sufficient reason why just that one exists. Yet it is clear that the sufficient reason for this world's existence cannot be contained within it, in nature.

Must we then abandon the principle of sufficient reason? Each part of nature has its sufficient reason in some other part of nature: in its cause at least, perhaps also in its purpose if it has one. And that sufficient reason has its sufficient reason in some other part; and so on . . . ad infinitum? It appears that if we stay within nature, we must either come in the end to at least one brute fact (maybe the "big bang" of the astrophysicists) or one "brute law" (maybe a unified field theory); or else we are confronted with an infinite regress of sufficient reasons, such that no reason is absolutely sufficient, only relatively so. In any case, as we have just seen, nature cannot contain within itself the sufficient reason for its own being, considered as a whole: in particular, why should there not have been just nothing at all? If we confine ourselves within nature in our search for a reason for nature, assuredly we shall find none; the totality of things will have to be taken as one stupendous brute fact; and as a brute fact it will be unintelligible, irrational.

Perhaps it is so. Perhaps the principle breaks down. Perhaps existence, at base, is a surd, and there is no use trying to adequate it to the intellect. Perhaps we must make shift to comprehend only the parts, never the whole.

However, let us not give up so easily. Let us at least ask ourselves what a sufficient reason for the whole might be like, if there were one.

We see immediately that it could not be a cause in the mechanical sense. The attempt to explain everything, whether piecemeal or all at once, in terms of a cause obviously leads us into an infinite regress—just what we are trying to escape. There remains for investigation, then, the possibility of finding a sufficient reason that is a choice.

Are we not faced here at the outset with the same difficulty of infinite regress? For we have already admitted that choices have causes. So that if the sufficient reason for the world were a choice, we could still ask for the cause of the choice; and so on.

But, after all, the choices that we are familiar with are made by limited, contingent beings. We must not be led too hastily to generalize on the sole basis of them. Rather, let us consider, within the sphere of human activities, what are the criteria by which we judge the adequacy of any explanation made in terms of a choice. That is, if we are told that X is as it is because P chose it to be that way, we may demand a further explanation of the choice—the choice itself may puzzle us. But perhaps not always: maybe sometimes this kind of answer is satisfying in itself.

Now it seems that we go on the following principle: we assume that a person makes the best choice he can. If his choice does not strike us as being the best possible, we wonder why it was not, and we search for reasons for the failure; but insofar as it is the best, we demand no further explanation. For the choice seems to us perfectly rational. Let me illustrate.

Someone builds a house of cheap materials, in a run-down neighborhood, not even taking advantage of the best available site on his lot; the rooms are poorly arranged and ventilated; the style is grotesque. We ask: Why did he do this? We answer: He couldn't afford anything better; he is not clever at design, and he was brought up by an ignorant and vulgar aunt. In view of his limitations, that was the best he could do. If a wealthy, ingenious, and well-educated person built such a house, we should perhaps have to conclude that he was not quite sane; we should think it fruitless to search for reasons for such behavior, and should engage rather in a clinical investigation of the causes of his psychosis.

If, however, a man of wealth and taste builds a convenient and beautiful mansion, we are not puzzled at all. That is just what one would expect; that is the rational thing to do. No doubt, there are causes of his being wealthy and tasteful; but those causes, whatever they are, are of only secondary relevance at most in explaining the house. It is sufficient that the house is the result of a rational choice.

Now let us suppose, for the sake of argument, that the world is the outcome of a choice. Is there any kind of choice that would in itself put an end to all puzzlement—that would not tempt us to ask further questions about the causes of the choice?

If we follow our homely example, it seems that this condition could be satisfied only if the choice were an absolutely rational one. And to be absolutely rational, to be self-sufficient as an explanation, the choice would have to be made by a Being subject to no limitations. If the chooser lacked power to produce whatever he wished to produce, we should want to know what prevented him. If he lacked the knowledge of all the alternatives, we should need to explain this lack. If, having complete knowledge and power, he nevertheless did not make the best choice, that would be most puzzling of all; we should call his behavior irrational and demand a cause. But if the chooser were subject to no limitations of power, if he chose in full knowledge of all the alternatives (all the logically possible ones), and chose the best—then this choice would be absolutely rational and would in itself constitute the sufficient reason for the world's being so and not otherwise. Since we have eliminated causes, and choices not fulfilling these conditions, only such a choice by an omnipotent, omniscient, and benevolent Being could be the sufficient reason for the universe.

Therefore if nature is rational, God exists. But there is good reason to believe that nature is rational: to wit, all of science and the rest of experience. Therefore there is good reason to believe that God exists.

This completes the exposition of the subtle cosmological argument, which in ingenuity and elegance perhaps marks the high point of rational theology. A few points concerning it remain to be noted:

First, it is not appropriate to ask, "Who made God?" and "What are the causes of the infinite Being?" in this context. God, as sufficient reason for nature—chooser of its laws as well as of its furniture—must be outside nature; but it is only within nature, i.e., within a framework of causal presuppositions, that it makes sense to ask for causes.

Second, God is the necessary Being in the sense of our definition of this term: a Being not dependent on the existence of anything else for His existence; not such that He could be otherwise in any respect, whatever else were the case. This is not to say that God's existence is logically necessary, in the sense that His nonexistence is inconceivable. One can conceive of there being no universe at all and no God. One can (perhaps) also conceive of the universe being irrational, hence either the result of the choice of some small-*g* god or of no choice. The argument claims only that God, as the source of all being, including all causation, cannot conceivably be Himself limited by any causes—in other words, there cannot be any cause (or indeed any reason) why He should not exist. Only in this sense does His essence entail His existence.

Third, the word "choice" in this context must of course not be supposed to carry with it any connotation of an act in time. The choice of "the best" by God is not to be thought of as the result of long and painful deliberation; this would be inconsistent with omnipotence. Hence the argument is neutral with respect to the issue whether nature has a beginning or not. (Or is this quite true? Theologians since St. Augustine have been aware of the difficulty involved in the notion of a temporal world brought into existence by a timeless Being: if the sufficient reason for the world is eternal, must not the world be eternal? If not, there must have been a time when the sufficient reason existed, but what it was the sufficient reason *for* did not. This is still another problem that we shall pass by as not relevant to our main concern.)

Fourth, as Leibniz noted,[15] it follows as a corollary that this is the best of all possible worlds. The reader is begged

[15] *The Principles of Nature and of Grace, Based on Reason* (1714), sec. 10.

to withhold his Voltairean laughter, pending discussion in due course.

Summary of the Argument

1. There is a sufficient reason why everything that is, is so and not otherwise. That is, wherever there is a plurality of logically possible alternatives, there is a sufficient reason why the alternative realized is the one realized.

2. Sufficient reasons are either causes or choices or both.

3. Of any cause, as distinguished from choice, one can always legitimately ask what its cause is.

4. Hence causes cannot be ultimately sufficient reasons.

5. Now the actual universe is not the only possible universe.

6. Hence (by 1, 2, and 4) its sufficient reason must be a choice.

7. But choices are sufficient reasons only insofar as they are rational choices.

8. A choice is rational insofar as it is choice of the best; and insofar as limitations of power or knowledge are imposed on the chooser, the choice is rational only relative to these limitations and requires further explanation.

9. Therefore an absolutely rational choice, requiring no further explanation, is a choice of the best, made by a Being subject to no limitations.

10. Therefore (by 5, 6, 9, and the definition of God) God exists.

Criticisms of the Argument

1. *The Problem of Evil.* "O Dr. Pangloss! If this is the best of all possible worlds, what must the others be like?"[16] This is a serious objection; but Leibniz and many other phi-

---

[16] Voltaire, *Candide*, ch. 6.

losophers and theologians have not thought it insuperable. They have argued that the evil that exists is necessary for the sake of a greater good. "Best of all possible worlds" does not mean "world without evil in it"; it means "world in which there is the greatest possible surplus of good over evil." We shall defer discussion of this matter until we come to the argument from design, in connection with which the same problem arises.

2. *Does choice presuppose a chooser?* In the presentation of the argument, we have assumed that whenever anything is explained as being the outcome of a choice, there must have been an intelligent personality who made the choice. And of course in our experience of choices, this is always so. It may seem, then, that we have raised a foolish question.

But we have noted that the choice of the world by God must be radically unlike any human choice, in that it is not an act in time. Although we have excused ourselves from probing the difficulty this raises of reconciling the argument with the doctrine of creation, there is another worry that we cannot avoid. It is this: the sufficient reason for this world being the actual one is (according to the argument) that an infinite Being recognizes it to be the best possible, and consequently actualizes it—the recognition and actualization not necessarily being processes in time. Now I for one can form no clear notion of what nontemporal recognition and actualization might be like. But we need not dwell on this mystery. The question is, rather, this: Is the sufficient reason demanded by the argument to be found only in the recognition and actualization? Or would it not simply consist in this world's *being* the best possible? In other words, should we not deem the requirement of a sufficient reason for the world to be fully satisfied if we found it to be the case that this world is the best possible? The world itself, that is, might be the necessary Being after all: infinite in power and maximal in goodness, but neither containing nor presupposing any personal intelligence, the function of which would be only to perform the mysterious nontemporal acts of recognition and actualization. The world might be conceived of as having (nontemporally) actualized itself—more simply, as having just always been here, so to speak, automatically. It is hard to see why the argument should not lead to this conclusion just as well as to the more orthodox one; the former would seem preferable on grounds of economy, particularly since it would dispense with the hard notions of nontemporal acts and supernatural Being. This is in fact the conclusion that Spinoza (who was not hampered by the necessity of defending any orthodoxy) *did* reach;[17] indeed even Leibniz was horrified to see himself being forced toward it.[18]

As far as I can see, the only way to obviate this theologically unwelcome conclusion is by argument to the effect that the unified complexity of the world requires, as its source, a separate and equally unified complexity, which would have to be in some sense a personal intelligence. In other words, the cosmological argument cannot stand alone as a proof of the existence of a personal God, but must be supplemented by the argument from design.

3. *What guarantee is there that the universe must meet the requirements of reason?* We have already had occasion to note that the argument does not really prove unconditionally the existence of God. It only offers us this dilemma: either God or an ultimately irrational universe. Brute facts, we may grant,

[17] Spinoza, *Ethics*, Pt. I, *passim*; but cf. especially Def. 6, Props. 16, 18, 29, 32, 33, and Appendix.

[18] See the correspondence with Arnauld; cf. also Bertrand Russell, *A Critical Exposition of the Philosophy of Leibniz*, ch. 15.

are not intelligible; but does it follow from this that there are no brute facts? What reason have we to believe that the universe is so accommodating?

One might say that we cannot know in advance that it is, but nevertheless we do have good reason to believe it: the principle of sufficient reason, so far from being whistling in the dark, is confirmed in everybody's experience all the time, and in more recondite regions of inquiry by the continual triumphs of science. Yes, but on closer scrutiny it appears that at best what is confirmed by experience and science is the causal principle—which is just that portion of the principle of sufficient reason that is rejected in the argument as being without possible application to the reason for things in general. The utmost that our experience teaches us about choices as sufficient reasons is that a vanishingly small fraction of the occurrences in an infra-infinitesimal part of the universe are such that our puzzlement about why they are as they are may be provisionally resolved by the knowledge that they are the outcome of intelligent choice—and only provisionally, for in no such case that we know of is it senseless to ask after the causes of the choice (though sometimes it may not serve our practical purposes to make the inquiry). It is a gigantic leap from here to choice as a cosmic principle—choice, moreover, so radically different in nature from anything we are acquainted with that to use the word "choice" is presumptuous.

Besides, the spectre of an unintelligible universe, with which the argument menaces us, turns out not to be so frightening a haunt when we get closer to it. We make progress in understanding the world by relating one part of it to another via causal laws; and we relate one law to another via more inclusive generalizations. No doubt the ideal is to reduce to a minimum the residue of brute fact and brute law; but surely it would be an exaggeration to maintain that unless the possibility exists of reducing this residue to zero, all our efforts are in vain. Suppose word were flashed to all the laboratories of the world that it had at last been proved, beyond any peradventure of doubt, that an infinite Being, the sufficient reason for the world, exists: what help could this news conceivably be for any research in progress? If the bulletin announced instead the definitive triumph of atheism, would any project have to be abandoned? Individual scientists might be elated or depressed at either report; that is all.

4. *Is it meaningful to ask, "What is the sufficient reason for the whole universe?"*

Our previous three criticisms suggest that there are cracks in the structure of the argument; this one questions the solidity of its foundation.

Logicians warn us against a certain mistake in reasoning, which they call the fallacy of composition. This error consists in arguing that since every member of a collection has a certain property, therefore the collection itself (as a whole) must also have the same property. Stock examples: every player on the team has a mother, therefore the team has a mother; everything heavy falls if not supported, therefore the earth would fall if it were not held up by something. Is not this fallacy committed in arguing: There is a sufficient reason why everything that is, is so and not otherwise; therefore there is a sufficient reason why the universe (i.e., the collection of all things) is so and not otherwise?

But the WHOLE, you say, wants a cause. I answer, that the uniting of these parts into a whole, like the uniting of several distinct counties into one kingdom, or several distinct members into one body, is performed merely by an arbitrary act of the mind, and has no influence on the nature of things. Did I show you the particular causes of each individual in a collection of twenty particles of matter, I should think it very unreasonable, should you afterwards ask me, what was the cause of the whole twenty. This is sufficiently explained in explaining the cause of the parts.[19]

But one must not lightly charge the great logician Leibniz —to say nothing of the Scholastics—with an elementary blunder. It is not always a matter of rote application of a simple rule to discover whether or not this fallacy has been committed. For instance, it is not committed in the following: Every resident of this community is wealthy; therefore this is a wealthy community. Besides, the argument explicitly states a reason for demanding an explanation of the universe: to wit, that it is not the only possible world. We must go somewhat more deeply into the matter. We must reopen our discussion of the nature of explanation.

The primary purpose of explanation of any sort is the elimination, or at least reduction, of puzzlement and uncertainty with their attendant fears. Let us consider first what kind of puzzlement causal explanation removes, and how.

Think of life as a game we play with nature. Success in this game, as in most others, depends on our being able to anticipate our opponent's next move—on the ability to tell from what is happening now what is likely to happen next. To do this we must discern patterns in the operations of nature, connecting events at one time with other events at other times. These patterns we call causal laws; they state that when, and only when, conditions of the kind C are fulfilled, events of the kind E will occur. A causal explanation is an argument of this form:

E-events occur only in C-circumstances (causal law).
E_0 is an E-event that has occurred (final condition).

---

[19] David Hume, *Dialogues concerning Natural Religion* (1779), Pt. IX.

> Therefore conditions C_0 must have obtained (initial condition or inferred cause).

For example:

> Only when the water supply is contaminated with the bacillus *Vibrio comma* does a cholera epidemic occur.
>
> A cholera epidemic is now occurring in X.
>
> Therefore the water supply in X is contaminated with *Vibrio comma.*

This last is only an expansion of what is contained in the statement "The citizens of X are suffering from cholera because their water supply is contaminated." Of course there is no warrant for calling it *the* explanation of the epidemic; we may want to know how the water supply got infected; or we may want to know more particulars of the process intervening between the contamination and the outbreak. That is to say, a causal chain of indefinitely many links is involved. But each link is expressible in the same form: causal law, final condition (report of observation, phenomenon to be explained), and inferred cause (initial condition, deduced from the preceding two statements).

Prediction differs in form from explanation only in that the minor premise of the argument states an initial rather than a final condition:

> In C-circumstances, E-events occur.
>
> Conditions C_0 are realized (initial condition).
>
> Therefore event E_0 will occur (final condition, prediction).

For example:

> Whenever war breaks out, the birth rate increases.
>
> X and Y have declared war on each other.
>
> Therefore the birth rates in X and Y will increase.

Every causal explanation requires two elements: a causal law, which as such mentions no particular occurrence at all; and a statement describing a particular occurrence (final condition, that which is to be explained). From these together we deduce a description of the initial condition (particular cause). But if every event has a cause, then the initial condition is itself the final condition in some other explanation, some other link in the causal chain. Hence causal explanation, by its very nature, always generates an infinite regress.

We have reached this conclusion in focusing our attention on the minor premises of explanatory arguments, the statements of particular conditions. But not only are events explained in terms of preceding events; laws themselves are explained in terms of more general laws. Inhalation of carbon monoxide causes death because the carbon monoxide combines with hemoglobin, rendering it incapable of absorbing oxygen. More formally:

> Whenever hemoglobin is rendered incapable of absorbing oxygen, death ensues.
> When carbon monoxide is brought into contact with hemoglobin, the hemoglobin is rendered incapable of absorbing oxygen.
> } Laws of Wider Scope
>
> Therefore when carbon monoxide is inhaled, death ensues (law of narrower scope, which was to be explained).

This procedure does not generate an infinite regress; theoretically, the end of the process comes when a law is enunciated broad enough in its scope to cover all lesser laws as particular instances. This condition is approximated in physics. If the supreme law were discovered, clearly it would be senseless to ask for an explanation of it—at least for an explanation in the sense just described.

We now see how causal explanation "eliminates alternative possibilities," how it shows us that such-and-such must be so and not otherwise. Here is E_0; might it not just as well have been F, or G, or . . . ? But now E_0 is explained: the explanation is to the effect that all C's are followed by E's, and there was C_0, therefore there had to be E_0 and not something else. The "must," then, is the "must" of logical necessity: it is logically impossible (literally inconceivable) for the explanatory premises to be true and the conclusion false. But this necessity is only relative to the premises, which are not in themselves necessary. The particular premise may be itself necessary relative to some other set of premises, but unconditional necessity is never attained. As for the major premise, the statement of a law of nature: might nature not have had some other law? No, because the law is explained, that is, deduced from a more inclusive law; and if that more inclusive law holds, then it is logically impossible for the restricted law not to hold. It logically cannot be the case that both *(a)* all interference with oxidation of hemoglobin results in death, and *(b)* carbon monoxide, when inhaled, interferes with oxidation of hemoglobin but does not cause death. But as in explaining events, so also in explaining laws we do not and cannot arrive at unconditional logical necessity. The most general law that we know is, by the very fact of its being the most general law, unexplained; and even in principle some law must ultimately remain unexplained. And if it is unexplained, it has no kind of necessity, and we may ask, if we like, why it should not have been otherwise. But if we ask this, we ought not to be disappointed that no answer is forthcoming. This is no defect in causal explanation; it is not the case that causal explanation is failing to do something that we might reasonably expect it to do.

All this is to show more particularly why it is that causal

explanations can never yield a sufficient reason for the universe at large. To put it in a slightly different way, the universe is the framework within which causal explanations operate. And although these explanations show the linkage of one part of the universe to another, it is quite beyond their scope to link the universe to anything else. To ask for the cause of the universe is to ask a question similar to "When is time?" or "Where is space?"

It may seem odd that I labor these points in a section supposedly devoted to criticism of the cosmological argument, since it is just these points that the argument insists on, as disposing of any claim of causal explanation to be ultimate. The purpose of going over these matters will become clearer as we proceed. At present what I want to show is that causal explanation really does do what it is intended to do; further, that it is misleading to say, "There are some things that it cannot explain," if this be taken as suggesting that by some other hook or crook the things might get explained. But let us go on.

Causal explanation and the prediction it facilitates alleviate puzzlement and fear. If we know that conditions C lead to disaster, then, when we observe C_0, we can take to the hills; further, when we know that D leads to C, and D is controllable by our efforts, we may eliminate D, if we have time. Intellectual, or idle, curiosity may make us wonder what the causes of D are; and if we have nothing better to do, we may investigate them. There is no limit to the lengths to which we may push the inquiry. We shall never come to a cause necessary in itself, but that does not disturb us, either practically or theoretically—unless we are metaphysicians; in which case the proper remedy for our puzzlement on this score is to get clear about why it is senseless to ask for ultimate causal explanations.

So much for causes. Let us turn now to purposive explanation, and begin likewise by asking what the aim of this kind of account is.

We have already answered this question in a general way: the aim is to remove puzzlement, uncertainty, and fear. But those contexts in which purposive explanations are known to work are restricted to human activities plus perhaps some activities of certain other animals. What kinds of puzzlement, uncertainty, and fear concerning human beings and their actions do purposive explanations intend to eliminate?

Let us go at this question indirectly, via our previous example of the house. We saw that if the house is perfect, we require no explanation at all; it would not even occur to us to ask for one. The imperfections are what demand explanation: what puzzles us is why the house is not as good as it might be. Removing puzzlement by producing an explanation in terms of choice consists in doing some or all of the following: (*a*) pointing out that the house was the best that could be built, considering the limitations imposed by circumstances over which the designer had no control; (*b*) showing that the design best serves the builder's purposes, which were not understood by the critic—showing, moreover, that these purposes are reasonable ones: it would not ordinarily do to say, "I wanted a house where there were the maximum number of things to bang my head on"; (*c*) showing that even though, from an objective standpoint, the design will not do at all, still, considering the builder's deficiencies in taste and ingenuity, he did the best that could be expected. (The builder would not say this, but someone else might, and it would count as an explanation.)

This kind of explaining is better called justifying or excusing. We think it worthwhile to justify or excuse our behavior, because we have a decent respect for the opinions of mankind; we solicit such justifications and excuses from other people, because when we do not have them we feel doubt, uncertainty, and fear: fear that the other people can't be counted on, that we shall not know what they are going to do next. What we do expect is rational behavior. I do not mean to say that we are all naively idealistic; rather, this is the norm, if not the statistically normal. Conformity to this norm requires no explanation; departure from it requires justification to show that the departure was only apparent, or excuse to show that it was unavoidable. And that is why, when we are convinced that something resulted from choice of the best, we are satisfied and ask for no further explanation.

Purposive explanation is not a rival of causal explanation. It is not something that does well what causal explanation does poorly, or that could take over the job at the place where causal explanation breaks down. It is an entirely different activity; the only overlap of the two kinds of explanation is that both are expedients for removing puzzlements—but quite different kinds of puzzlements.

Applying these results to the cosmological argument, we must conclude that the reasoning "The universe can't be explained causally; therefore if it is to be explained at all, it must be explained purposively" really rests on a sort of pun: as if one were to say, "This patient can't be cured in a hospital; therefore if he is to be cured at all, he must be cured in a smokehouse."

What has not been explained is why, if the cosmological argument rests on a pun, the fact has gone unnoticed by some rather penetrating thinkers. But this is not hard to understand. The type of explanation of the universe at large that is offered really is, and really is intended to be, a justification of the universe. It is offered to alleviate some very real fears: fears that the cosmos is not to be counted on; not operating to produce the best; unsocial and unsociable. In sum, fears that the cosmos is "irrational"—but irrational not in the sense in which an unexplainable event or law is brute or irrational, but as a man who cannot justify or excuse his conduct is irrational. To these fears the cosmological argument brings the reassurance that, appearances to the contrary notwithstanding, *this is the best of all possible worlds.* What is formally only a corollary of the argument is really the heart of it.

"If the universe is justifiable, then God exists." If we restate the argument in line with our criticisms, this much remains. I see no reason for quarreling with this proposition. All the same, to the question "Does the cosmological argument afford any reason for believing that God exists?" our answer must be negative.

Yet . . . why *is* there anything at all?

The Argument from Design

UNLIKE the ontological and cosmological arguments, which are mostly the preserves of theologians and philosophers, the third member of the traditional triad is of great popular appeal. In skeleton outline it is this:

1. Nature everywhere exhibits orderly structures and processes.
2. Orderly structures and processes are always the work of intelligent personality.
3. Therefore nature is the work of an intelligent personality, i.e., of a god.

The Psalmist sang: "The heavens declare the glory of God; and the firmament sheweth his handywork."[20] This, the central thought of the design argument, is virtually as old as humanity. Naturally the argument has been stated in numerous forms, which differ among themselves according to what orderly structures and processes are regarded as especially significant, and with respect to the means adopted for proving the second premise, that order presupposes intelligence.

[20] Psalms 19:1.

The evidences for order in the world are derived from our experience of nature; and in general the argumentation in support of the second premise (which I shall refer to hereafter as "the design axiom") purports to show that it too is a generalization warranted by experience. Thus the argument, it is claimed, has the same form as scientific argument or as inference from circumstantial evidence in judicial proceedings: "Here is the evidence, visible to everyone; we need to account for it; and the only hypothesis, or at least the most plausible one, that will account for it is that of a god. Nature is orderly; but if there were no god, nature (if there were any) would in all likelihood be a mere chaos; therefore there is a god."

I say "a god," not "God," conceding at the outset the objection that our experience of the causes of order at best can never show that any organization whatsoever has to be the production of a single and infinite personal intelligence. The argument from design cannot prove, by itself, monotheism as against polytheism; nor can our finite experience of finite kinds and amounts of orderliness, however vast in scale, establish the infinity of its cause. Moreover, our experience of order is always of the imposition of organization on pre-existing materials; thus the argument from design cannot by itself prove, or render probable, the creation of the world out of nothing. This is not to say that the argument disproves, or tends to disprove, the existence of God. The argument is neutral on this point: God's existence is compatible with it, but not necessitated by it. (This seems so prima facie. However, we shall have to consider later, in connection with the problem of evil, an argument which professes to show that the existence of God is in fact incompatible with the existence of nature as we know it.)

The argument from design thus differs from the other two

traditional arguments in being an induction from factual evidence, whereas the ontological argument wholly, and the cosmological argument almost wholly, are products of "pure reason." Unlike the latter two, it aims to show only that there is at least one small-g god; and it can do no more than demonstrate this conclusion to be highly probable, not logically necessary. It does not follow, however, that the design argument is the weakest of the three, only that it is more modest in its pretensions. It purports to offer us the kind of evidence that would be accepted in a physical laboratory, or in a court of law. Surely it would be finicky to reject as of no account argumentation for the existence of a god that establishes that inference as firmly as the physicist proves the existence of electrons, or as the prosecuting attorney showed that Bruno Hauptmann murdered the Lindbergh baby. And this is the kind and degree of proof that supporters of the design argument claim for it.

Moreover, if there is a god—and the argument, if it proves anything, proves the existence of a rather august deity— then the further step to the existence of God is in practice a short one, even though one might say that theoretically it is infinite. If there exists an intelligence so stupendous as to be the effective source of the whole organization and harmony of the universe, it would be overly nice to grumble that monotheism remains to be proved.

Sketch of the History of the Argument

At least four stages can be distinguished in the development of the design argument. I shall call these the primitive, the teleological, the clockwork, and the entropy stages.

1. *The Primitive Stage.* Here the argument is not yet explicitly formulated, for the good reason that arguments are not constructed to prove beliefs that no one conceives of doubt-

ing. When primitive man, "having dined" (Rousseau[21]), begins to think about the origins and guiding forces of nature conceived more or less as a whole, he does not "reach the conclusion" that nature is the product of manlike beings; he does not, that is, consider various alternatives and hit on this one as the most likely. Rather, the conception of an impersonal force or agency does not occur to him—not because he is obtuse, but because, first, there are only a few cause-effect relationships known to him in which his experience encompasses both the cause and the effect: hunting, canoe making, pottery, sorcery, etc.; all or nearly all of these involve personal agency. Second, primitive thinking is conducted in social terms, for the idea of the individual contrasted and possibly opposed to the social unit has scarcely arisen—and in social terms, the question that is asked about any event that needs accounting for is not "What caused it?" but "Who is guilty?" It would be misleading to describe primitive thought as conceiving of all causes as personal, for our notion of cause is simply not present. It is better to say that all primitive explanations consist in imputing guilt or responsibility.[22]

Since, furthermore, primitive man recognizes no sharp boundaries between himself, his tribe, and nature, it is inevitable that his thinking about nature will be in social terms. Thus the question "Is nature ordered and controlled by persons?" is not asked; one only asks specific questions about the identities and characteristics of the controllers. To these questions mythologies provide the answers. Primitive man, we may

[21] Jean-Jacques Rousseau, *A Discourse of the Origin of Inequality*, Appendix.

[22] This account of primitive thinking, which is perhaps obvious a priori, is abundantly confirmed by anthropological investigations. See, e.g., the summaries and references in Hans Kelsen, *Society and Nature* (Chicago: University of Chicago Press, 1943).

note, does not seem much concerned with problems of the literal truth of his myths. Nor need we concern ourselves with the matter. What we must emphasize is that the framework of primitive thought excludes from consideration any interpretation of nature other than a personal one. To primitive mentality, the questions "But really, *is* there a being—a being with thoughts, loves, hates, and power—who hurls the lightning? Might not the lightning 'just happen'?"—these questions would be very strange, perhaps incomprehensible; just as physicists early in this century found strange the suggestion that perhaps they could not find the cause of the disintegration of a radium atom because that event had no cause.

2. *The Teleological Stage.* In the primitive stage, there is no design argument, because there is no occasion for it. There is a world outlook that finds verbal expression in mythology, and that goes beyond particular myths to dominate the whole mode of thinking. This world outlook is personal, animistic. No one bothers to set it out, so to speak, in a textbook; there is no need to do so. Probably the textbook could not be written in any case, for one could not say intelligibly to one's audience that "the world is the abode of personal forces" unless the contrary of the statement would make some sense to them.

Only in response to the challenges of objectors, innovators, and subverters does the textbook get written. The Psalmist, besides assuring us that the heavens declare the glory of God, also complains, most significantly, "The fool hath said in his heart, There is no God."[23] In Western thought, the doubts and alternative hypotheses—of the world being as it is because of the operations of impersonal fate or chance or "fortuitous concourse of atoms"—were put forward by the

[23] Psalms 14:1; also 53:1.

Ionian Greek philosophers of nature, beginning with Thales and culminating with Democritus. The response, the reintroduction into serious and advanced thought of the notion of cosmic purpose and personality, was the work of Anaxagoras, Socrates, Plato, Aristotle, and the Stoics. The philosophies of these men comprise sophisticated world outlooks in which teleology is central: one's understanding of the world, or indeed of anything in it, is declared to be incomplete unless one grasps the relevant purpose or goal. The claim of the nature philosophers, that understanding consists in knowledge of causes (in the modern sense of the word), is not rejected, but held to be incomplete. Thus according to Aristotle's celebrated doctrine of "four causes" we understand a thing only if we know what it is made of: the material cause; who or what made it, and how: the efficient cause (roughly, "cause" in the modern sense); its form (shape or activity): the formal cause; and its end, that which it naturally tends to become, its *raison d'être:* the final cause, its *telos.* Of these four, all but the first, according to Aristotle, are really aspects of a single notion, the essence of the thing, its purpose and the fulfillment of that purpose.[24]

All this is a far cry from wood nymphs, thunder gods, and Marduk and Osiris making their mud pies. And in fact, belief in a superhuman organizer who conceives the cosmic project and carries it out by forming the originally chaotic matter of the world, as a potter moulds his clay—this belief was held only halfheartedly or perhaps in a figurative sense by Plato,[25] and not considered at all by Aristotle and the Stoics. Stoicism is pantheistic in holding that God is the soul of the world, an aspect of it, not outside it, and not personal, except in a very attenuated sense. Aristotle's god moves the

[24] *Metaphysics* V, 2.

[25] *Timaeus, passim.*

world through the intricate evolutions of the spheres only "as the beloved moves the lover,"[26] or as the goal posts move the football players; though his pure activity is thought and he is a personal god in the sense of being a unitary intelligence, he makes nothing, nor is he even aware of the world.[27]

In consequence, the argument from design had no place in Aristotle's theology, which was based instead on the cosmological argument.[28] And while the Stoics expatiated upon the orderliness of the cosmos, their inference was that since the universe, like the human body, is organized, so also it must have a soul; but this doctrine is pantheism, not personal theism. Thus in antiquity, the design argument declined in relative importance. It is instructive to consider why the decline was only temporary.

Philosophically, what had happened was that these thinkers had tried to retain the notion of purpose while doing away with the proposer. What remained was a sort of grin without a cat, which could not long endure. Theologically, or rather religiously, the excogitated deities (or divine aspects) were of no use, because of their depersonalization and consequent lack of interest in and responsibility for the affairs of men. Hence it is not surprising that the general run of even cultured men came to prefer the grossest superstitions to the abstractions served up by the philosophers.

Christianity asserts the existence of a personal creator and designer. But original Christianity was not a philosophical system at all, and propounded no arguments. Thus Aristotelian metaphysics and Christian religion each lacked what the other could provide. We see through hindsight that it was inevitable for the two to unite; though the union had to wait

---

[26] *Metaphysics* XII, 7

[27] *Ibid.*, 9.

[28] *Ibid.*, 6; *Physics* VII-VIII.

until the twelfth century for its consummation. Aristotle's cosmological argument supplied, for St. Thomas Aquinas, the principal rational means for demonstrating the existence of God; but since the Christian God, not the Aristotelian *theos*, was shown to exist, it was appropriate for St. Thomas to reintroduce the design argument:

The *fifth way* is taken from the governance of the world. For we see that certain things which lack consciousness, such as natural bodies, act for an end; this is evident from their acting always, or rather often, in the same way, so as to obtain the best result. Hence it is plain that not by chance, but by intention, do they achieve their end. Now whatever has not consciousness does not move toward an end unless directed by some being endowed with consciousness and intelligence; as the arrow is shot by the archer. Therefore some intelligent being exists by whom all natural things are directed to their end; and this being we call God.[29]

The Aristotelian contribution to this version of the argument is the premise that all things "act for an end," and the support of this premise, "this is evident from their acting . . . in the same way, so as to obtain the best result." St. Thomas departs from the Philosopher in arguing further that the movement toward an end must be the result of direction by "some being endowed with consciousness and intelligence, as the arrow is shot by the archer"—in Aristotelian words, there must be an intelligent efficient cause, applied *ab extra*, to account for orderly processes. This is not to say that the regulators (Aristotelian "entelechies") of orderly action—the nesting instinct of birds, the gravitation ("seeking its natural place") of stones, the perfect circular motions of celestial spheres—may not be, so to speak, "built in"; however, the Saint insists that if they are built in, some intelligent being

[29] *Summa Theologiae*, Pt. I, Ques. II, Art. 3; tr. by the author.

must have built them in. Everything orderly must have an intelligent efficient cause—our design axiom. St. Thomas does not argue in support of this axiom; it is self-evident for him.

3. *The Clockwork Stage.* The Aristotelian system was based on animism, but the edifice was so elaborate that the foundations were hardly visible; and in fact the principal support, the design axiom, was removed altogether. St. Thomas strengthened the whole by putting this pillar back; nevertheless, other weaknesses eventuated in collapse, in the seventeenth century.

I shall not relate the story of this debacle. For our purposes it is sufficient to note that Galileo and Newton did away with the idea that motion (and consequently other kinds of change, if there are any) required some explanation of its persistence; in Newton's system only changes in the direction or speed of motion need be accounted for. Second, change of motion was to be accounted for, and accounted for completely, in terms of force, two varieties of which were recognized: impact of one body on another, and gravitational attraction. Both of these were measurable and impersonal; description of events in these terms rendered superfluous the notion of Aristotelian final causes. That is, final causes disappear because their principal function, in the Aristotelian system, was to explain why things left to themselves do not come to a dead halt; while in the new science uniform motion was as "natural" as rest. Nor could the Aristotelian system be patched up by invoking final causes to explain nonuniform motion. In the Newtonian system acceleration was fully explicable in terms of the interactions of forces communicated from one body to another by impact or gravitation. The latter force had been purged of the connotation of "seeking natural place," for Copernicus, Kepler, and Bruno had abolished the absolute center of the universe.

We must emphasize, however, that only strictly Aristotelian final causes—internal sources of motion and change, built-in purposes not entailing a planner—were excluded from the new mechanical philosophy. Final causes, in the wider sense of purposes *ab extra,* were not eliminated from scientific thinking in one fell swoop. It was then, and perhaps still is, rather audacious to speculate that every kind of event, including the phenomena of life and consciousness, is amenable to mechanical explanation. The more advanced thinkers admitted that final causes had no place in explaining any change that could be analyzed without remainder into a complex motion of particles; but they by no means regarded it as certain that every event was of this kind.

But although final causes and purposes are easily confused, they are really distinct notions; hence the abolition of the former did not entail the extinction of the latter from the world outlook. Final causes are at the heart of the cosmological argument; cosmic purposes are of the essence of the argument from design. The principal effects of the scientific revolution on natural theology were as might have been expected: de-emphasis of the cosmological argument, with a tendency to revert from the subtle to the crude form, and elevation of the relative importance of the argument from design. Less was heard of immediate providence (it became incredible, for instance, that comets, whose orbits had been calculated, should be divine portents), and compensatingly more of the necessity of a god as original designer of the harmonious universe.

For, it was thought, there are two kinds of order, and the mechanical philosophy can explain only one of them. There are aggregates, and there are organizations. When a volcano erupts, boulders of various sizes and shapes are strewn about the landscape—all in strict accordance with the laws of motion and of gravitation. Some peasants come along, select stones of the right size, dress them, and make a wall of them. The muscular forces that they have to apply to lift, transport, and chip the stones are also mechanically explainable. None of the laws of motion would have been violated if the forces in the volcanic eruption had been just right to deposit the whole collection of boulders, not as a heap, but as a wall in the first place. Nevertheless, volcanic forces are "blind"—they might produce an organization, but they seldom do. On the other hand, the forces exerted by the peasants' muscles are purposefully directed; they ordinarily produce organizations rather than aggregates.

Now if nature were nothing but the playground of blind forces, nature should be (so the argument goes) wholly, or almost wholly, composed of aggregates. But in fact it is full of organizations, very many of which exceed in fineness, intricacy, and ingenuity any production of human purposiveness. Here is where mechanical explanation shows itself incomplete: not that anything in nature is necessarily incompatible with, a "violation" of, the laws of motion; but these laws of themselves cannot account for the amount and kind of organization that is to be found. Nature is a cosmos, not a chaos; but it is so probable as to amount almost to certainty that a nature that was the product only of the forces inherent in matter would be a chaos. Hence nature must have been organized from outside, by the only kind of force we know to be capable of producing organization: purposive intelligence.

Newton himself wrote in this vein:

The six primary planets are revolved about the sun in circles concentric with the sun, and with motions directed towards the same parts, and almost in the same plane. Ten moons are revolved about the earth, Jupiter and Saturn, in circles concentric with them, with the same direction of motion, and nearly in the planes of the orbits of those planets; but it is not to be conceived that mere mechanical causes could give birth to so many regular motions, since the comets range over all parts of the heavens in very eccentric orbits. . . . This most beautiful system of the sun, planets, and comets, could only proceed from the counsel and dominion of an intelligent and powerful Being. . . . [Though we have no adequate idea of God's attributes,] we know him by his most wise and excellent contrivances of things, and final causes. . . . Blind metaphysical necessity, which is certainly the same always and everywhere, could produce no variety of things. All that diversity of natural things which we find suited to different times and places could arise from nothing but the ideas and will of a Being necessarily existing. . . . And thus much concerning God; to discourse of whom from the appearances of things, does certainly belong to Natural Philosophy.[30]

The perfect example of a mechanical system is, of course, a machine; and to the eighteenth century the most fascinating kind of machine[31]—the only one, besides the harpsichord, allowed in the drawing room—was the clock. Here is a complicated assemblage of parts, each interacting with all the others, directly or remotely, not capriciously or confusedly but with the regularity for which the word "clockwork" has become a synonym. The whole concerted action serves a purpose, the purpose envisaged by the clockmaker; the organization would not exist but for that purpose, and for the intelligence that designed and made that elegant instrument out of aggregates of raw materials. The classical statement of the argument from design, by "Cleanthes" in Part II of Hume's *Dialogues con-*

---

[30] *Principia* (1687), tr. Motte, Bk. III, General Scholium; quoted in T. V. Smith and M. G. Grene, eds., *From Descartes to Kant* (Chicago: University of Chicago Press, 1940), pp. 375-378.

[31] It is odd in English, though not in French, to call clocks "machines." They are, rather, mechanisms. However, the classic statements of the argument ignore this fact, and no harm seems to come of it.

cerning Natural Religion, draws an analogy between the universe and a machine:

Look round the world, contemplate the whole and every part of it: you will find it to be nothing but one great machine, subdivided into an infinite number of lesser machines, which again admit of subdivisions to a degree beyond what human senses and faculties can trace and explain. All these various machines, and even their most minute parts, are adjusted to each other with an accuracy which ravishes into admiration all men who have ever contemplated them. The curious adapting of means to ends, throughout all nature, resembles exactly, though it much exceeds, the productions of human contrivance—of human design, thought, wisdom, and intelligence. Since therefore the effects resemble each other, we are led to infer, by all the rules of analogy, that the causes also resemble, and that the Author of nature is somewhat similar to the mind of man, though possessed of much larger faculties, proportioned to the grandeur of the work which he has executed. By this argument *a posteriori,* and by this argument alone, do we prove at once the existence of a Deity and his similarity to human mind and intelligence.

In its cultural context, this formulation of the argument was a very strong one, appealing even—or especially—to men who rejected most of the tenets of orthodox religion. It was the crushing retort to atheists: in Coleridge's famous lines,

> Forth from his dark and lonely hiding-place
> (Portentous sight!) the owlet Atheism
> Sailing on obscene wings athwart the noon,
> Drops his blue-fringèd lids, and holds them close,
> And hooting at the glorious sun in Heaven,
> Cries out, "Where is it?"[32]

Hume's trenchant criticism of the argument, usually considered definitive, was in fact limited in its scope. He concerned himself principally with showing that the analogy on

[32] "Fears in Solitude" (1798).

which the argument rests (or appears to rest: see pp. 122 ff.) is weak—for the universe is not very much like a machine; that the argument generates a vicious regress—for we are entitled to ask after the material basis of the cosmic intelligence; that the argument at best cannot prove the unity, infinity, benevolence, or even continued existence of a deity; and that it "affords no inference that affects human life, or can be the source of any action or forbearance."[33] The design axiom itself, however, was still left standing, though wobbling, at the end of the *Dialogues:* "the cause or causes of order in the universe probably bear some remote analogy to human intelligence."[34]

4. *The Entropy Stage.* Hume could not demolish the design axiom, for want of an alternative hypothesis to account for cosmic order. Not quite seriously he suggested "generation" as an alternative principle of ordering, revealed in experience; and he speculated that the universe might be as well compared to an animal, or even a vegetable, as to a machine. That would not do, of course, since "generation"—a process the mechanisms of which were entirely unknown in Hume's day—was precisely the principal fact that design was invoked to explain.

In the middle of the nineteenth century, Darwin and Lyell provided the alternative hypothesis that would account mechanistically for biological order. While the Ionian Greeks had developed evolutionary speculations to an astonishing extent, Aristotle had rejected their conclusions, and on this subject his authority, later reinforced by Genesis, stood unchallenged for more than two millennia. This fact should be borne in mind when assessing the plausibility of the design argument before Darwin: even Hume was obliged to assume that either the present array of living things had eternally existed in all its

[33] *Dialogues*, Pt. XII.
[34] *Ibid.*

complex variegation, or else everything had come into being all at once and together.

After 1859, it was possible to regard the curious adapting of means to ends in nature as the outcome of a long process of development, in which, beginning with the simplest kinds of proto-organisms, those varieties that just happened to possess some slightly superior adaptation to their environment—some little added fillip of complexity—would survive and reproduce themselves, passing on their advantage to their descendants, while their inferior rivals became extinct. Darwin in biology, like Laplace in celestial mechanics half a century earlier, "had no need of the hypothesis"[35] of God.

The furious attacks on Darwinism in the nineteenth century were motivated chiefly by desire to preserve the literal interpretation of the Scriptures. In the long run, however, the danger posed to traditional theism by Darwinism was more fundamental: it lay in the undermining of the design axiom. In our own day the new science of genetics has shown how both slight individual differences and major mutations come about, while Darwin's principles still suffice to account for the change in character, over a long period, of a population in which variations occur—the "origin of species."

It should not, however, be concluded too hastily that 1859 marked the demise of the argument from design. Recently, attempts have been made to rehabilitate this argument by showing that the process of evolution itself, being progressive in character, is inexplicable unless a guiding intelligence is postulated. Two related inferences are urged in support of this conclusion. One purports to be derived from the statistical theory of probability: the universe, big as it is and old as it is, is still not big enough or old enough for there to be a

[35] Laplace's reply when asked by Napoleon why there was no mention of God in his *Mécanique Céleste*.

significant probability of organizations as complex as those found in living things being formed by mere planless mixing. The other comes from the second law of thermodynamics (law of increase of entropy), according to which (so it is argued) all merely mechanical processes move in the direction of greater disorganization, whereas evolutionary processes, which show the opposite tendency, must in consequence be other than merely mechanical.

At the present time, the question whether the argument from design offers a reasonable basis for belief in the existence of a god is very much the same as the question whether the probability and entropy considerations lend any support to the design axiom. I shall therefore examine these arguments in greater detail.

The Probability Argument

Human Destiny (1947), the last work of the French physiologist Pierre Lecomte du Noüy, contains the best-known recent presentation of the probability argument. In summary it is as follows:

Life has not always existed on this planet. The origin of life was either the result of the working of intelligence in some sense, or it was not. If it was not, then it happened "by chance alone," i.e., as the result of fortuitous concourse of atoms moving randomly.

Now one essential constituent of all living things is protein. The simplest protein molecule contains about 2,000 atoms of five different kinds; and it is not just an aggregate of these atoms, but an intricate organization of them.

For the sake of simplicity, assume that a simple protein molecule consists of 2,000 atoms, and of two kinds only, not five. Assume further that the structural complexity of the molecule can be represented by degree of dissymmetry 0.9.

("Dissymmetry" is a measure of separation of distinct constituents. Thus a bottle of milk in which all the cream is at the top exhibits the maximum degree of dissymmetry, i.e., 1; while homogenized milk has 0 dissymmetry.) Professor Charles-Eugène Guye has calculated the probability of a chance occurrence of a configuration of these specifications. It is 2.02×10^{-321}, i.e., two chances out of a total number that would be represented by 1 followed by about six lines of zeros on this page.

The volume of substance necessary for such a probability to take place is beyond all imagination. It would be that of a sphere with a radius so great that light would take 10^{82} years to cover this distance. The volume is incomparably greater than that of the whole universe including the farthest galaxies, whose light takes only two million years to reach us. In brief, we would have to imagine a volume more than one sextillion, sextillion, sextillion times greater than the Einsteinian universe.

The probability for a *single* molecule of high dissymmetry to be formed by the action of chance and normal thermic agitation remains practically nil. Indeed, if we suppose 500 trillion shakings per second, which corresponds to the order of magnitude of light frequencies . . . , we find that the time needed to form, on an average, one such molecule . . . in a material volume equal to that of our terrestrial globe is about 10^{243} billions of years.

BUT WE MUST NOT FORGET THAT THE EARTH HAS ONLY EXISTED FOR TWO BILLION YEARS AND THAT LIFE APPEARED ABOUT ONE BILLION YEARS AGO, AS SOON AS THE EARTH HAD COOLED.

Life itself is not even in question but merely one of the substances which constitute living beings. Now, one molecule is of no use. Hundreds of millions of *identical* ones are necessary. . . .

We are brought to the conclusion that, actually, it is *totally impossible* to account scientifically for all phenomena pertaining to Life, its development and progressive evolution, and that, unless the foundations of modern science are overthrown, they are unexplainable.[36]

Du Noüy was not so incautious as to conclude at once that since it is totally impossible to account scientifically (i.e. mechanically) for life, therefore the existence of God is proved. More modestly, he contented himself with the inference of "telefinalism," that an "anti-chance factor" must be at work in the universe. Quite understandably, nevertheless, apologists for theism greeted Du Noüy's book as a vindication of their position, a turning of the tables on "materialists," who were thus shown to be the real believers in miracles. As our author permitted himself to remark:

The writer is not naive enough to think that this discussion will convince any materialist. People who have a faith cannot be convinced by mere words and logic. Men with an irrational faith— and we hope that we have made it clear that such is their case— do not yield to rational arguments.[37]

Criticism of the Probability Argument

It is not wise, however, to believe that an argument is irrefutable just because its author says so. In the present instance the "rational argument" rests on an untenable assumption, and the "logic" leads to an unwarranted conclusion. For the only thing really proved, granting the calculations, is the fantastic improbability of any protein molecule ever having come into existence all at once as the result of the simultaneous combination of its simple atomic constituents. But no "materialist"— at least, none since the fifth century B.C.—ever dreamed of anything of this sort.

[36] Pierre Lecomte du Noüy, *Human Destiny* (New York: Longmans, Green, 1947; Signet ed., 1949), Bk. I, Pt. 3, Signet ed., pp. 35-37; quoted by courtesy of David McKay Co., Inc.

[37] *Ibid.*, conclusion of Bk. I, p. 46.

Let us make a further simplifying assumption and talk not of protein molecules but of adult human beings. We are justified in doing so, because while a human body is more complicated than a protein molecule, the latter is already so incredibly complex that the figure for the improbability of the "chance" production of a human body is scarcely more staggering than the protein figure given us by Guye and Du Noüy.

In these terms, which may be pictorially somewhat more vivid, the alternative posed by Du Noüy becomes this: either human bodies are the products of intelligent design, or else they are the results of atoms somehow coming together, in their haphazard motions, in just the right way.

About 440 B.C., the physician-philosopher Empedocles accepted this dilemma; and since he believed that everything came about by "mixture and separation," he took the second horn. His speculation about the origin of life was that the earth, at a certain period, spontaneously produced all kinds of monsters and *disjecta membra:*

Where many heads grew up without necks, and arms were wandering about naked, bereft of shoulders, and eyes roamed about alone in need for foreheads.[38]

Many creatures arose with faces and breasts on both sides, offspring of cattle with human faces, and again there sprang up children of men with cattle's heads; creatures, too, in which were mixed some parts from men and some of the nature of women, furnished with sterile members.[39]

Of these chance productions the only ones to survive were the very few that were so organized as to be able to live and reproduce.

The principle of Empedocles' reasoning—"survival of the

[38] Fragment 57 (Diels's numbering).
[39] Fragment 61.

fittest"—is that of modern evolutionary theory; but his detail is fantastic. We may say that Du Noüy has thoroughly refuted him—but him only. For it is another principle of evolutionary thought, equal in importance to the survival of the fittest, that nature makes no leaps. The chance agglutination of atoms into fully formed men, or protein molecules, would not be evolution but its antithesis. The evolutionary concept is that just as man is the last stage reached to date of an immensely slow and complicated process of successive modifications in less complex creatures, so also the protein molecule itself is the resultant of a very large number of successive stages of synthesis, beginning with quite simple compounds.

Chemists have long been able to synthesize very complex compounds in the laboratory. The first synthesis of proteins has recently been announced. To be sure, laboratory procedures are instances of "telefinalism," the chemist's manipulations being the "anti-chance factor." It is more relevant, however, to observe that the synthesis of a complicated compound always proceeds in the laboratory in steps. One does not make even so simple and common a compound as acetic acid just by mixing up its constituent carbon, hydrogen, and oxygen. We must leave it to the French to calculate how many sextillions of sextillions of sextillions of years that would take. Instead, one takes some lime (calcium oxide) and heats it with carbon to produce calcium carbide, which then reacts with water to yield acetylene. This can be oxidized to produce acetaldehyde, and further oxidation of the latter compound yields acetic acid. But every step in this process consists in bringing certain ingredients together at certain pressures and temperatures, whereupon the desired reaction occurs spontaneously.

The acetic acid that occurs in nature is the product of a far more complicated process—involving, as a matter of fact, the action of proteins. But the same considerations apply. We may, if we like, stupefy ourselves at the fantastic improbability of the "chance" occurrence of acetic acid out of its atomic constituents, *tout court*. But that would be nothing to the point. The "probability" of acetic acid being formed in nature is not this probability, but the product of the probabilities of conditions permitting the steps of the synthesis to be realized in succession.

But is it meaningful at all to speak of probabilities in such contexts? This brings us to the unwarranted assumption of Du Noüy's argument. He states it in this way:

Let us define what is understood by the *probability* of an event: it is the ratio of the number of cases favorable to the event, to the total number of possibilities, *all possible cases being considered as equally probable*.[40]

This amounts to what statisticians call the "principle of indifference" or the "principle of insufficient reason": if there are *n* possibilities, and we know of no reason why one should be more likely to occur than another, then the probability of each is $1/n$. It is sometimes said that we assume this principle when we declare the probability of throwing double six to be $1/36$; for there are thirty-six ways in which two dice can fall, only one of which is "favorable to the event," and we know no reason why any one of the thirty-six possibilities should be more likely than any other. Even here, though, the application of the so-called principle is dubious. Is it not, rather, that all those who concern themselves with the probabilities of dice have at hand a great deal of antecedent knowledge about the behavior of symmetrical objects? And what if nonloaded dice inexplicably kept falling double six—would we go on saying that the probability was still just $1/36$? In any case, the general application of the principle would yield some very

[40] *Op. cit.*, p. 31.

curious results. For instance, we know nothing of the causes of baldness. We know, then, of no reason why any person should, or should not, be bald; consequently the probability that any person—young or old, male or female—is bald is the same as the probability that he is not bald. Therefore it is a matter for astonishment that only a small fraction of human beings are bald (and there must be a cosmic hairdresser at work?). And we know of no reason why the star Sirius should have, or should not have, a planet. Therefore, the probability that Sirius has a planet is 1/2. Moreover, we know of no reason why it should, or should not, have a hundred planets. Therefore the probability that Sirius has a hundred planets is 1/2, and identical with the probability that it has just one planet. The principle of insufficient reason is only one more fairly ingenious attempt to distill knowledge out of ignorance.

The conception of probability employed by most statisticians is that of relative frequency in the long run. The probability that a given individual will be bald is just the number of bald persons, divided by the total number of persons, bald and hairy. If our livelihood depends on probabilities (if we are insurance actuaries, say) we shall choose the best-defined reference class we can in making our estimate: if we have to make a bet on whether Jones will die in the next ten years, we shall not content ourselves with using the mortality rate for the general population, but will want to know the age, sex, race, personal habits, medical history, etc., of Jones; and we shall make our estimate on the basis of the class containing individuals who approximate Jones in these characteristics, which are antecedently known, by experience, to be relevant to longevity. If we cannot get the information about Jones, then the best we can do is calculate the probability relative to the whole population; if we happen to have no statistics about that, then we can assign no probability at all. We may make a random guess; but that is not the same thing.

How probable is it that Sirius has at least one planet? Many, perhaps most, statisticians would refuse to speak of such a "probability"; but if there is one, it is equal to the number of stars, in a significantly large random sample of stars, which have each at least one planet, divided by the total number of stars in the sample. Since we have no adequate sample of stars to go by, we do not know at all what the probability is. Indirectly, we may approach the problem by finding out something about cosmic evolution; but that is another matter, though it may still involve probabilities, in relation to another kind of reference class. The principle of insufficient reason, however, is not to be invoked.

The question "What is the probability of proteins developing 'by chance'? " is an extremely complicated one—supposing it to make any sense at all. To answer the question adequately, we would need to know in the first place what the successive steps are in the natural synthesis of proteins out of basic constituents. But after leaping that formidable hurdle, we would still need a lot of other information hard to come by, such as the value of the probability that a given planetary atmosphere will at some time be composed principally of ammonia and methane. (The formula "Number of planetary atmospheres containing ammonia and methane, divided by total number of planetary atmospheres," though correct, is no help.) Indirectly, statistics which astrophysicists can obtain about the relative abundances of carbon, hydrogen, and nitrogen in the universe provide some very slight basis for estimating this probability; but in general we may say that we have no data at all on which to base an estimate of the probability of "chance" occurrence of protein.

If we did have the answer, it would be of no interest to us.

We would merely know, then, that we live on a rare planet, or on a common one, as the case might be. Knowledge of the statistical probability would not of itself entail any knowledge of the causes.

It should not be supposed that if Du Noüy's version of the probability argument fails, some other such argument might succeed. If in the present state of our cosmic knowledge there is no way of selecting a reference class so as to make a meaningful estimate of the probability of life beginning "by chance," then it is not possible even to state any version of the probability argument without assuming the principle of insufficient reason. Or in other words, every such argument must be vitiated by the initial fallacy of deciding a priori what is probable and improbable, or (what amounts to the same thing) of confusing the wonderful with the improbable. Of course, the origin and development of life on this planet is an awe-inspiring theme. By no means does it follow that the process cannot have an explanation of the usual scientific sort.

Since the actuarial concept of probability is of no help in estimating the chance of protein, or men, occurring from "random shuffling of atoms," we may choose to invoke some other notion of probability: for instance, we may define probability as the measure of rational expectation. But if we do, then we should remember that it is reasonable to expect things to happen as they do happen; and that is all there is to say about the matter.

The arguments based on "the fitness of the environment"[41] resemble the probability argument in dwelling on the complex concatenation of "improbable" characteristics that matter in general, and the earth in particular, must have in order to render life possible. If the earth were only a few million miles closer to the sun, or farther away from it, the climate would be too hot or too cold; or if the earth did not revolve as it

[41] For exhaustive examples see the publications listed in note 48.

does, with the angle between the polar axis and the ecliptic being just what it is, the climate would be extremely unpropitious; or if water did not exhibit the anomalous behavior of expanding upon freezing, the oceans would all be frozen, etc. Such arguments, however, amount to regarding this world, with the laws of nature operative in it, as only one of the infinite "possible worlds." In effect, they bid farewell to the argument from design and return us to the cosmological argument.

The Entropy Argument

There is another modern form of the argument from design which, while it has much in common with Du Noüy's, appeals not primarily to the mathematical calculus of probabilities in order to make its point, but to a well-established generalization of physics: the second law of thermodynamics (law of increase of entropy).

The law can be stated in various ways. Perhaps the most common statement is this: in any isolated system, entropy tends to a maximum. Now entropy is not a concept that is easy to grasp intuitively. It can be defined precisely only in terms of the integral calculus. Very roughly, the entropy of a region (spatial volume) is the amount of heat energy in the region divided by the temperature of the hottest object in the region.[42] If the region is isolated, that is, if no energy flows into it or out of it (a tightly stoppered thermos bottle approximates this), the second law of thermodynamics states that the

---

[42] A little less roughly: for a given spatial region, if Q is the quantity of heat measured in calories, T the temperature of the hottest body measured in degrees Kelvin, and S the entropy,

$$S = \frac{Q}{T}$$

If S_i is the entropy of the initial state of some isolated system, and S_f the entropy of the final (or any later) state of the same system, then

entropy cannot decrease; it must either remain the same or grow larger. This does not mean that the temperature of the hottest body in the isolated region, or indeed of the whole region, may not increase: for example, a fire may break out in it. According to the law, however, even in that case the increase of energy in the form of heat must outstrip the rise in temperature.

All this may seem remote from natural theology. The connection will begin to be visible when we observe that what the law states, abstractly and precisely, is that all things left to themselves tend to "run down." For the entropy of a system is a measure of the amount of energy in the system that is unavailable to do work. By the law of conservation of energy, the total energy in an isolated system remains constant. Energy may exist in various forms, however: coiled springs, electric cells, gunpowder, fire, etc. Suppose an ice chest contains initially air and a battery-operated electric fan. This array will run for a while, then stop. But there is still as much energy in the chest as at the beginning. What has happened to it? It existed at first as chemical potential energy in the cells of the battery; this was converted into electrical energy, the directed flow of electrons in a wire; the motor converted it into mechanical energy, rotation of the armature and fan blades—and finally the fan blades stirred up the air, that is, imparted additional *random* motion to the air molecules, this random motion constituting an increase in the amount of heat in the air. But that is the end of the line. There is no way of reversing the process and using the random motion of the air molecules to

the second law of thermodynamics is: the quantity $S_f - S_i$ is always either zero or positive,

$$S_f - S_i = \frac{Q_f}{T_f} - \frac{Q_i}{T_i} \geq 0$$

For a precise statement, see any textbook of physics.

turn the fan blades, to operate the motor as a generator and recharge the battery. The energy which at the beginning was available to do work (turn the fan) has now been rendered unavailable, dissipated, "degraded." The entropy has reached a maximum, and nothing further can happen as long as the chest is closed.

The only way to extract work from heat energy is to have two bodies at different temperatures and utilize the flow of energy from the hotter to the colder. But the process entails the heating of the colder and the cooling of the hotter. If left to itself, the system must reach thermal equilibrium, the point at which the two bodies are at the same temperature and no more work can be done. The molecules are still moving, but moving at random—as many, on the average, in one direction as in another. Their motion, at first organized and hence available to do work, is now disorganized. When a wind is blowing, i.e., when most of the air molecules are moving in the same direction, a windmill can be operated; when the air is still, the molecules are still moving, nearly as fast individually as in the wind, but their motion will not now actuate any mechanical device.

From this we may conclude (but with a caution to be emphasized later) that the entropy of a system is a measure of its disorganization, and we may rephrase the second law to read: any isolated system tends to become more and more disorganized.

The application to the design argument should now be apparent: nature, left to its own devices, runs down. Two inferences are drawn: first, nature must have been "wound up" in the first place by some outside force; second, those processes within nature that show increase of organization cannot be "merely natural," but must be somehow under the guidance of an extranatural organizing force. Now the only such organizing force we know is mind; therefore we must postulate a cosmic mind as director of the evolutionary, i.e. progressive, processes in the universe.

In his book *Belief Unbound* William Pepperell Montague defended theism by a combination of the probability and entropy arguments. Montague's version of the latter runs this way:

The law of increase of entropy holds universally, "in any world in which there is random motion alone, or random motion supplemented by such reciprocal *ab extra* determinations as are formulated in the laws of physics."

And yet within this world that is forever dying, there have been born or somehow come to be, protons, and electrons, atoms of hydrogen and helium, and the whole series of increasingly complex chemical elements culminating in radium and uranium. And these atoms not only gather loosely into nebulae, but in the course of time combine tightly into molecules, which in turn combine into the various complicated crystals and colloids that our senses can perceive. And on the only planet we really know, certain of the compounds of carbon gain the power of building themselves up by assimilation, and so growing and reproducing. Life thus started "evolves," as we say, into higher and higher forms, such as fishes, reptiles, and birds, mammals, primates, men, and, among men, sages and heroes.[43]

This tendency to organization, contrary to the otherwise universal entropic degeneration, is not plausibly to be explained "with only the types of mechanistic causality . . . that are recognized in physics."

But what is the alternative . . . ? Nothing so very terrible; merely the hypothesis that the kind of causality that we know best, the kind that we find directly and from within, the causal-

[43] William Pepperell Montague, *Belief Unbound* (New Haven: Yale University Press, 1930), pp. 70 f.

ity, in short, that operates in our lives and minds, is not an alien accident but an essential ingredient of the world that spawns us. . . . We merely suggest that the kind of anabolic and antientropic factor of whose existence we are certain in ourselves, is present and operative in varying degree in all nature. If we are right, we escape the universe of perpetual miracle, on which the atheist sets his heart.[44]

In summary:

1. All merely physical processes are entropic.

2. All entropic processes tend to dissolution and disorganization.

3. Therefore all merely physical processes tend to dissolution and disorganization.

4. But some processes—namely, evolutionary ones—tend to synthesis and organization.

5. Therefore some processes are antientropic and not merely physical.

6. Now we know that mind is an antientropic factor; and mind is the only antientropic factor we know.

7. Therefore evolutionary processes are probably mind-directed.

The main things wrong with this argument are that the sixth premise is dubious and the second is certainly false. Let us begin by discussing the sixth premise.

A common example of increase of entropy is the diffusion of liquids. Half fill a beaker with water and then very carefully pour red wine into the upper half. There will then be two layers, the bottom one colorless and the top one red. If the beaker is left undisturbed, in time the differentiation will vanish; a uniformly pink fluid will be found in it. This is be-

[44] *Ibid.*, p. 73.

cause the molecules of water and wine[45] at the boundary are in constant random motion, some up, some down. The molecules of wine will pass into the water, and vice versa. The process is not reversible; separate layers of wine and water will mix themselves up, but no mixture of wine and water will separate itself.

Strictly speaking, the latter eventuality is not impossible, only highly improbable. For the second law is a law of statistically average behavior. At some time all the wine molecules just might happen to be moving upward, while simultaneously all the water molecules happened to be moving downward. The chance of such an occurrence, however, is represented by the rather French number of one in 1,550 sextillions, if the beaker holds one quart.

But suppose now that a solid disc is placed horizontally in the middle of the beaker. There is a hole in it just big enough to allow a single molecule to pass; and the hole is provided with a cover. This cover is held by an infinitesimal but intelligent being ("Maxwell's demon") who is able to distinguish water molecules from wine molecules, as in their random motion they approach the hole. Whenever he sees a wine molecule approaching from below, or a water molecule from above, he opens the hole and lets the molecule pass through; otherwise he keeps it shut. In this way the mixture might separate itself (for the demon does not *shove* any of the molecules; he does no work on this isolated system), and its entropy might decrease under the guidance but not added physical energy of an intelligence.

What this hypothetical case shows is that a pure, i.e. disembodied, intelligence could conceivably be an antientropic factor. But it is a dizzy leap from this to the conclusion that the intelligence we have is antientropic. Sorting, to be sure, is

45. I need hardly say that "molecule of wine" is a *façon de parler*.

a typical intelligent activity. The oranges come down the chute; the sorter (a man or a machine) causes the good ones to roll to the right, the culls to the left. However, if the sorter is a machine, it is constantly degrading electrical and mechanical energy into heat; if a man, he is doing the same with carbohydrates and proteins. The "isolated system" here cannot exclude the sorter and its energy needs. A machine sorter that would degrade no energy is impossible. I shall not dogmatize that a mind independent of a material and entropic structure is out of the question, but it cannot be seriously maintained that we know of the existence of any such entity. There is no "anabolic and antientropic factor of whose existence we are certain in ourselves."

Montague seems to overlook the fact that the second law applies only to total entropy in an isolated system. There is nothing to forbid the entropy of some *part* of a system being decreased, and in fact this is very common. A steam generator, burning coal and producing electricity, is upgrading energy. A man lifting a rock onto an elevated platform is doing the same. All that the law requires is that the amount of energy degraded in the whole process should exceed the amount upgraded; and there is no reason to believe that this requirement is not satisfied in both cases—not to mention more spectacular examples such as the synthesis of proteins by plants, in which the "isolated system" must be regarded as including not only the plant and its immediate environment, but the sun also.

However that may be, the argument is certainly vitiated by its second premise, that all entropic processes tend to dissolution and disorganization. "Disorganization" is a vague term; nevertheless, most people would presumably regard H_2O as more "organized" than H_2 and O_2, cream-on-top-and-milk-below as more organized than mixed cream and milk, stars as more organized than clouds of cosmic dust. Yet the processes whereby these "organizations" come into being exhibit increase in entropy no whit less than "levelling, scattering, and disorganization." From the standpoint of thermodynamics it is as Heraclitus said: the way up and the way down are one and the same.

If this were not so, the second law would be a scientific monstrosity. The laws of science have no exceptions—not because of the strictness of their enforcement, or the wisdom of scientists, but just because if a real contrary instance to an alleged law is discovered, the law ceases to be a law (more exactly: "We thought it was a law, but we were mistaken"). If evolutionary and other anabolic processes—of which physicists are hardly unaware—were antientropic, the second law of thermodynamics would long since have been discarded or explicitly limited in its scope. It would have to read, in effect: all processes occurring in an isolated system are such as to increase the total entropy of the system, except for those that decrease it. To put it another way: Montague, in effect, has claimed to have discovered that the second law of thermodynamics is false. And the fact that the literature of physics contains no discussion of this claim should hardly be taken as indicating a cowardly conspiracy of silence.

There is one plausible though not certain inference to be drawn from the second law, which may have some bearing on the question of the existence of God. If the universe can be considered as an isolated system (this is questioned by Hoyle and other "steady-state" cosmologists), and its entropy is constantly increasing, then, extrapolating backwards, there must have been a time in the remote past when that entropy was zero, or at least very small. And several independent lines of evidence converge in pointing to something extraordinary having taken place about eleven billion years ago. A creation out of nothing, by an infinite Being if you like, is a hypothesis that cannot be ruled out by the physical evidence presently available. But neither is it in any degree confirmed by that evidence, nor is it the only possible hypothesis.

The Design Axiom Considered Further

It would be a mistake to think that Du Noüy and Montague have bungled jobs that others might do more skillfully. For any attempt to show that the basis on which probabilities are to be calculated is improbable, or that nature is unnatural, is bound to fail.

While the fallaciousness of an argument does not entail the falsity of its conclusion, it ought to be admitted that repeated failures to offer any sound reasons for a belief create some presumption that the belief is false. Nothing more than a presumption can thus arise, however; in the case of the design axiom, there are counterpresumptions in its favor, which are perhaps so strong that even the complete destruction of all forms of the design argument could not offset them. But before continuing our discussion, let us see where we now stand with respect to the design axiom.

The universe is full of complex organizations exhibiting "curious adapting of means to ends." Our question is, how are these to be accounted for?

There are three (and, as far as I can see, only three) abstractly tenable hypotheses: Aristotelian, mechanistic, and teleological.

1. The order in the world might have existed eternally. Particular instances of order in the present would be the outcomes of pre-existing equivalent orders, and so on back ad infinitum. If we held this view, and also allowed that the cosmological argument is fallacious, there would be no need to account further for order at all. However, facts available to

us are incompatible with this hypothesis, which we therefore can omit from consideration.

2. Complex organisms—we can restrict our survey to living beings without loss of generality—might be the outcome of a progressive development from simpler organisms; and the simplest organisms might themselves have developed gradually from even simpler combinations of material constituents, so that in the whole procession from the atom to the theologian there is nowhere any gap. Scientists, not philosophers, must decide whether this is in outline the picture of what has in fact happened; but at any rate I shall assume that it is correct.

The philosophical question does not concern the facts. It is this: Is evolution able to account for itself in its own terms? The mechanistic answer is affirmative. Given some initial distribution of matter in the universe (and we need not raise the question where *that* came from), the inherent properties —essentially, the energy distribution patterns—of the elementary particles are sufficient to account for their building up into all the complexes presently encountered, including living and conscious ones. Thus organisms would be "chance" products of the shifting distribution of energy in the universe—"chance" in the sense of not being directed by intelligent foresight, though not chance in the sense of being lawless. Leucippus, the first great Greek mechanist, expressed this in the only words of his that have survived: "Nothing happens at random, but everything for a reason and from necessity."[46]

It is essential to the mechanistic view that although a complex can arise only from pre-existing parts, the parts can and sometimes do pre-exist dissociated from each other, and can and sometimes do unite spontaneously—that is, a complex ef

[46] Fragment 2.

fect does not always require an equally complex cause. There is occasionally something new under the sun, though what is new is made from what is old.

3. The teleological hypothesis, while admitting the facts of evolution, insists that these facts are not self-explanatory. The effect cannot exceed the cause; in particular, organisms must be, ultimately, the effects of causes at least as complex and ordered as they themselves; and those organisms possessing consciousness could not exist unless their pre-existing cause were itself conscious and purposive. This is not to deny that the particular material configurations may have been produced out of simpler constituents, but it is to deny that the union could be merely spontaneous and inherent in the parts. "Dead matter" could no more form itself into an amoeba or a theologian than lumber, nails, and wire could, without the activity of a carpenter, form themselves into a chicken coop.

But the teleologist, in admitting the facts of evolution, really abandons his case. He has admitted that as far as immediate causes are concerned it is possible—since it is actual —that highly organized structures can evolve "naturally" out of relatively unorganized materials. If he insists that the remote, unobserved, and unobservable causes of order must be intelligent, what possible justification for this view can he put forward? Is this not just the final retreat, to the limits of the universe, of the animism that once triumphantly occupied the whole of it? If you ask, soberly and seriously, for an explanation of the order in the universe (says the mechanist to the teleologist), you are asking for an account of the causes of that order. Well, here is the outline of that explanation; here are some of the details that go to fill it out; and if you want more, scientists are uncovering them faster than you can assimilate them. What more can you ask for? To go on saying: but the ultimate cause of order must be orderly, the ultimate cause of adaptation must be purposive, the ultimate cause of consciousness must be conscious—to go on saying this is simply to betray the fact, suspected all along, that nothing will satisfy you but an animistic explanation; and this is a fact about your psychology, not a certain or probable inference about the nature of things.

Some Afterthoughts

Yet after the fallacies of the probability and entropy arguments have been exposed, and after the propensity to accept the design axiom has been ascribed to natural animism, the argument from design is but scotched. Its extraordinarily tough core continues to pulsate with life. That core is the impressive analogy between the universe and the products of intelligent foresight.

You will find [the world] to be nothing but one great machine, subdivided into an infinite number of lesser machines. . . . All these various machines, and even their most minute parts, are adjusted to each other with an accuracy which ravishes into admiration all men who have ever contemplated them. The curious adapting of means to ends, throughout all nature, resembles exactly, though it much exceeds, the productions of human contrivance. . . . Since therefore the effects resemble each other, we are led to infer, by all the rules of analogy, that the causes also resemble.[47]

Hume himself, after he had done all he could to expose the weakness of the analogy, grudgingly admitted that it has sufficient force to justify the conclusion that "the cause or causes of order in the universe probably bear some remote analogy to human intelligence." May we not still say that this is a matter of opinion, and that it is reasonable for us to hold

[47] Hume, *Dialogues*, Pt. II (see text, p. 99).

the analogy to be really strong and sufficient to validate the reasonableness of theism?

Perhaps we may, if the argument really establishes an analogy. But does it?

Stripped of rhetoric, the argument as presented by Hume (and accepted as a fair statement of it, by advocates and critics alike) is this:

Premise I. Natural objects share with artifacts the common characteristics of adjustment of parts and curious adapting of means to ends.

Premise II. Artifacts have these characteristics because they are products of design.

Conclusion. Therefore natural objects are probably products of a great designer.

In form this is an argument by analogy. The proponents of the argument maintain that the analogy is a strong one; the detractors judge it weak; all agree that the argument is an analogy.

Two curious circumstances, however, lead to the suspicion that this form misrepresents the gist of the argument. The first of these is that the dispute about this argument does not conform to the usual pattern of discussion of analogies in other contexts. Two examples will show what I understand to be the "usual pattern."

Are Australoids akin to Negroids? On the positive side are similarities in nose, lips, chin, leg-to-trunk ratio, pigmentation. Against the hypothesis are differences in hair, in brow, jaw, and forehead structures, and in predominant blood types. Anthropologists are agreed about the facts; although they may differ as to how much weight to assign to the inference, their differences are not very great. Anyone who thought the facts either prove or disprove the hypothesis conclusively would be regarded as a crank by his colleagues. All are agreed, furthermore, that if there were exact similarity in nearly all physical respects, if the two peoples told similar legends in languages of the same family, then there could be no reasonable doubt about it.

Was early Greek philosophy influenced by Indian thought? There is the featureless One of Parmenides, the metempsychosis of Pythagoras, Empedocles, and Plato, both of which conceptions are commonplaces of the "gymnosophists." On the other hand, there is a concern with nature, even in these putative Orientalizers, that is lacking or less emphasized in the East; it is plausible to suppose that ideas of these sorts are likely to crop up almost anywhere, etc. If the opposing viewpoints on the question have their devoted partisans, this may show only that philosophers are crankier than anthropologists. Here again, at any rate, it is agreed that if old Indian texts were discovered containing argumentation exactly parallel to that of Parmenides, if Greek inscriptions of the fifth century B.C. were shown to contain translations from the Rig-Veda, and so on, then a point would be reached at which the matter would be settled.

Controversy about design is conducted quite differently, as we have seen. Although there may be a fair amount of agreement about the particular facts of "adjustment of parts" and "curious adapting of means to ends," there is nevertheless violent partisanship in respect to the inferences to be drawn from these facts. The design proponents collect the evidences, and proclaim that any fool can plainly see what conclusion they inevitably lead to; the critics yawn and say it is no use going on like this, that no matter how many such curiosities are piled up, the inference is still inadmissible and must remain so. The analogy is weak, and no conceivable amount of further evidence of the same kind could strengthen it appreciably.

This is a curious circumstance. But since it may be explained away by reference to the importance of the subject, or to the peculiarities of philosophers and theologians, I do not lay great stress on it in isolation.

The second reason for doubting whether the design argument is an analogy is a weightier one. If the argument is an analogy, then it is an extremely weak one—much weaker even than Hume judged, so weak that we must be amazed that anyone could have thought it to have any force whatsoever. For it is in fact at least as weak as the following argument:

Premise I. Natural objects share with artifacts the common characteristic of being colored.

Premise II. Artifacts are colored by being painted or dyed.

Conclusion. Therefore natural objects are probably colored by a great painter-dyer.

I take it as self-evident that this is an extremely weak argument, to which no one would assent. Yet it cannot be weaker than the design analogy, because it is of the same form and its premises are obviously true. (It may be objected that the second premise is not true, since some artifacts retain their "natural" colors. I mean, though, that when we know how they got their colors, we know that they got them by being painted or dyed. And besides, some artifacts retain as components, "natural" adaptation of means to ends: e.g., squirrel cages.) How so weak an argument could seem strong needs accounting for; and I doubt whether cynical references to the unbounded credulity of *homo religiosus* will suffice.

I shall try to explain these anomalies by suggesting that the paint argument is less convincing than the design argument precisely because its premises are more obviously true. From this I shall conclude that the analogical form disguises the real form of the design argument.

If it were quite obvious—as obvious as that everything (not transparent) is colored—that everything has the property of curious adapting of means to ends, would there then be any temptation to argue that the cause of adaptation in natural objects must be like that in artifacts? I do not think so; but perhaps the thought-experiment is difficult and inconclusive. Let us go at it indirectly.

Suppose someone wanted seriously to urge the paint argument. One thing we can be sure of is that he would waste no effort on proving the first premise. It is obvious that everything, artificial and natural objects alike, is colored. No one would say: "Look here. Automobiles and billboards and books and wigs and so forth are colored, as you can plainly see. But look again and you will discern, on close inspection, that not only these but also peaches and strawberries and snow and the sky and natural hair and so forth are colored. Now, having established that beyond reasonable doubt, we can go on."

But this sort of thing is just what advocates of the design argument do at the greatest possible length. They take it for granted only that the curious adapting of means to ends is obvious where artifacts are concerned; they judge that the thesis they must devote their eloquence to convincing people of is the existence of adaptation in nature. In the heyday of the argument from design, books such as the eight volumes of the *Bridgewater Treatises*[48] were almost wholly devoted to establishing this fact. Their authors assumed, correctly, that they were presenting the public with information not otherwise available, and with inferences such as would not occur to just anyone.

---

[48] Eight books published 1833-1840 under the auspices of the Royal Society. The authors shared a legacy of £8,000 from the eighth earl of Bridgewater. In order of publication, they are: Thomas Chalmers, *The Adaptation of External Nature to the Moral and Intellectual Constitution of Man*; William Prout, *Chemistry, Meteorology, and the Function of Digestion, Considered with Reference to Natural Theology*; William Kirby, *The History, Habits, and Instincts of Animals*

Let us rewrite the argument in a way that will bring out this insistence on the nonobviousness of adaptation:

1. You can distinguish artifacts from natural objects; and you know two things about artifacts: first, that they exhibit curious adapting of means to ends; second, that they do so because they are consciously designed to do so. This you have learned from the experience of seeing them made.

2. If, then, you were to discover some object the origin of which was unknown to you, but which obviously resembled something else known to be an artifact, you would immediately, and correctly, infer that it too was an artifact and was the product of conscious design.

3. Now it is granted that natural objects, such as eyeballs and lizards, do not obviously resemble artifacts. But on closer inspection, they are seen to possess the essential characteristic of artifacts, that characteristic which when obviously present warrants an inference to design, namely, curious adapting of means to ends.

4. Therefore by parity of reasoning you should come to realize that natural objects too are products of conscious design.

This, I think, is a fair summary of the argument from design as it is actually argued (for example, by Paley[49]). Adverbs are often dispensable parts of speech, but not here. The

---

with Reference to Natural Theology; William Buckland, *Geology and Mineralogy Considered with Reference to Natural Theology;* Sir Charles Bell, *The Hand: Its Mechanism and Vital Endowments, as Evincing Design;* John Kidd, *On the Adaptation of External Nature to the Physical Condition of Man;* William Whewell, *Astronomy and General Physics Considered with Reference to Natural Theology;* and Peter Mark Roget, *Animal and Vegetable Physiology Considered with Reference to Natural Theology.*

[49] William Paley, *Natural Theology, or Evidences of the Existence and Attributes of the Deity* (1802).

gist of the argument comes in the third paragraph, and its force lies in the contrast between inspecting things superficially and inspecting them carefully.

There is nothing inherently illegitimate about argumentation of this form. It often happens that we divide a large class of things into two subclasses, those that have the property P and those that lack it—or so it seems; and then later we discover that really all the members of the class have P after all. Thus well into the nineteenth century biologists commonly divided living things into those that were generated from seed and those that were spontaneously generated. Then Pasteur showed conclusively that there is no such thing as spontaneous generation—all living things are generated from seed.

Reasoning of this kind is valid only when a division is made between two species on the basis of some clear and relevant criterion, such that things of one kind are found, on the evidence available, to satisfy it, and others are not; and subsequently it is discovered that the things thought not to satisfy the criterion really do. In the example, the criterion was a clear one: reproduction from germ cells provided by parent organisms. No one had discovered any bodies, produced by flies, mosquitoes, molds, etc., such that from them, and from them only, other organisms of the same kind would develop. All that was known was that in certain conditions (decaying vegetation, etc.) these flora and fauna seemed inevitably to develop. The criterion was clear, and the division in accordance with it was justified on the evidence available. It took ingenious investigation to demonstrate that in these cases too, seeds were present.

Does the reformulated argument from design conform to these requirements? Perhaps it satisfies the second. It is not obvious that very many natural objects, and features of nature, show fine adjustment of parts and curious adapting of means to ends; but closer scrutiny may establish this. And the criterion itself, though not so clear and easy to apply as that of presence or absence of seeds, may be conceded to be sufficiently definite.

The criterion assumed is the wrong one, however. Proponents of the design argument take it for granted that the properties according to which we judge whether or not some object is an artifact, are accurate adjustment of parts and curious adapting of means to ends. But that is not the way we judge, even provisionally, whether something is an artifact or not. This is clear from our being able to tell whether something is an artifact without knowing what it is for or whether its parts are accurately adjusted.

Suppose someone is given a heap of miscellaneous objects: watches, leaves, eyeballs, pistols, lizards, stone axes, sealing wax, abstract paintings, etc.; then suppose he is required to separate them into two piles, the one containing only artifacts, the other only "natural" objects. Anyone can easily do this. The reason why one can accomplish the task so easily, though, is perhaps just that one knows in advance which are man-made and which are not. So let us make the task more difficult. Let us put in the heap a number of "gismos"—objects especially constructed for the test by common methods of manufacture, i.e., metallic, plastic, painted, machined, welded, but such that the subject of the test has never seen such things before, and they do not in fact display any "accurate adjustment of parts" or "curious adapting of means to ends." Put into the heap also a number of natural objects which the subject has never seen. Will he have any more difficulty? He will not. The gismos go into one pile, the platypuses and tektites into the other, quite automatically.

Of course one might conceivably make mistakes in this

sorting procedure. And it is perhaps hazardous to predict that human visitors to another planet would be entirely and immediately successful in determining, from an inventory of random objects found on its surface, whether it was or had been the abode of intelligent beings. But space explorers would not be at a loss as to how to proceed in the investigation. They would look for evidences of machining, materials that do not exist in nature, regular markings, and the like. Presence of some of these would be taken as evidence, though perhaps not conclusive, of artifice.

This is how archaeologists decide hard cases. Is this object just a rock, or is it a hand ax? The scientist's inspection is not directed toward determining whether the object can serve a purpose; he looks instead for those peculiar marks left by flaking tools and not produced by weathering. Again: there is no question at all that Stonehenge is a human contrivance, though there is much controversy about its purpose.

We are now in a position to understand why the friends of Design go to so much trouble to show design in nature, and why the critics, blandly conceding all their opponents put forth, attack the argument at another point. Both accept the Humean formulation. For the advocate, the main job is to establish the first premise; once this is done, he thinks, the assimilation of natural objects to the category of machines follows immediately. The critic, on the other hand, goes to great lengths to resist this coalescence. His usual strategy is to show that the analogy—though proper in that natural objects and machines do both exhibit curious adapting of means to ends—is "weak," on the ground that the total disanalogy is great. But in taking this line the critic falls into the snare set by the advocate. Thus even such astute and skeptical inquirers as Hume and J. S. Mill[50] conceded some force to the de-

[50] John Stuart Mill, *Theism* (1874), "The Argument from Marks of Design in Nature."

sign argument. They need not have done so; for properly considered, the argument is not really an argument by analogy, strong or weak. It is just another argument with a false premise, and therefore of no force at all.

Part III

EVIL

The Argument from Evil

FOR the most part, opponents of theism take advantage of the debating rule that the burden of proof lies on the affirmative side. They content themselves with questioning the cogency of the reasoning urged by theists. There is only one argument offered as a positive reason for believing that God does not exist: that His existence is incompatible with the imperfections of the world.

1. If an infinite and perfect Being exists, then whatever else exists must be compatible with His will.

2. Only the existence of perfection is compatible with the will of a perfect Being.

3. The world is not perfect.

4. Therefore an infinite and perfect Being does not exist.

God is said to be perfectly powerful, knowing, and good. But there is evil in the world. Hence if God is omniscient and good, the evil must exist because He cannot prevent it; if so, He is not omnipotent. Or if He is omnipotent and good, the evil must exist because He does not know of it, and He is not omniscient. If, however, He both knows about the evil and is able to prevent it, but does not, then He is not good. Thus God may have any two of the traditional attributes, but not all three.

This classical formulation is ascribed to Epicurus, and is often referred to as the "Epicurean Paradox." I do not know why, for it has no more of paradox ("a tenet contrary to received opinion; also, an assertion or sentiment seemingly contradictory, or opposed to common sense, but that yet may be true in fact"—Webster) about it than the multiplication table. The common sense of mankind has regularly inferred, from the capriciousness and cruelty of nature, that the gods, the powers behind nature, must themselves be to some extent capricious and cruel—an inference strengthened by the fact that men, who furnished the pattern in terms of which the gods were conceived, are notably capricious and cruel. Religious practices have been frankly designed to secure advantages from the gods by techniques recognizing and exploiting their cupidity, selfishness, vanity, and malice. Nor are such features altogether absent from the observances associated with religions which formally acknowledge monotheism. The theology of the perfect Being is the innovation, the paradox. It is principally a heritage from Greek philosophy.

But this is neither here nor there, since we have decided that the general consent of mankind furnishes no cogent reason for believing—or not believing—in the existence of God. The only point in mentioning the matter at all is that it enables us to put the argument from evil in proper perspective. Two points need to be made.

First, if the argument is valid it does not prove, nor tend to prove, atheism understood as the denial of all and any supernatural personal existence. Although the existence of evil is compatible with an impersonal universe, indifferent alike to the joys and the sufferings of sentient creatures, it is equally compatible with a universe run by a committee of less-than-perfect gods, or by just two opposing forces, one good and the other evil (as in Manichaeism and some less exotic cults), or by one august but limited deity.

Second, the argument from evil is an argument in its own right. It is commonly presented as if it were just one more objection to the argument from design: that is, if the order and good in the world are relevant evidence for the existence of a benevolent designer, so by parity of reasoning the disorder and evil are relevant as contrary evidence. This is true, no doubt, but hardly worth mentioning except in rebuttal to an oversanguine presentation of the design argument. That argument, as we saw at the outset of our discussion of it, can never alone prove the existence of an infinitely perfect Being. Moreover, a sort of inverse, or perverse, design argument could be based on the evil in the world, or at least that considerable amount of it that is not identical with disorder. The line of reasoning purporting to show that strawberries and saints are improbable can be turned to the same office for mosquitoes and tyrants.

It is somewhat different with the cosmological argument, which if valid would prove the existence of God and would entail as a strict corollary that this is the best of all possible worlds. I have tried to show why the cosmological argument is invalid, and in doing so I made no use of inferences drawn from evil. This seemed to me the best procedure, because if one is convinced that the actual world is not the best of all possible worlds, then one must allow that something is wrong with the cosmological argument; but nothing is shown thereby as to just what it is that is wrong. Thus the argument from evil, considered as an objection to the cosmological argument, is either superfluous or relatively useless.

Explication of the Premises

1. If an infinite and perfect Being exists, then whatever else exists must be compatible with His will.

The assumption here is, of course, that an infinite and perfect Being would be a person and would have some aspect corresponding to what we call "will" in ourselves. He would be conscious, aware of alternatives, and would prefer some alternatives to others.

That God is a Being with a will in this sense is comprised in the definition of "God" adopted in this book—a definition which, as far as I can tell, is in accord with the tenets of all monotheistic religions, at least in the Western world. One is at liberty—philosophically—to adopt some other definition; and this has been done. For instance, Aristotle's God, while "perfect," was not infinite, since infinity (i.e., endlessness, hence incompleteness, hence disorder) was not congenial to classical Greek thought. Thus Aristotle's God was pure actuality, thought thinking of thought, but not a person, not someone having desires even in the sense of preferences, and not a creator. The gods of Epicurus were similar except that they were material and more given to sensuous enjoyment than to metaphysics. Such kinds of beings, however, are irrelevant to the theism we are discussing. That kind of theism accepts this premise. And also the next one:

2. Only the existence of perfection is compatible with the will of a perfect Being.

It is part of the concept "perfect Being" that such a Being, when aware of alternatives, prefers the best possible. Here "possible" means "logically possible." This is a somewhat different notion of possibility from the one with which we are acquainted in our ordinary affairs. (See the discussion pp. 58 ff.) *We* are not perfect beings, or at any rate not infinite ones, hence our choices of the best are conditioned by empirical limitations. The ideal housewife chooses the best menu possible on her budget, recognizing that what is most delicious is seldom what is most nutritious, and coming to some kind of compromise. An ideal and "infinite" housewife, however, could choose without regard to expense and could make her menu both perfectly delicious and perfectly nutritious: if the requisite foodstuffs did not exist already, she could create them *ex nihilo.* Or she could redesign the physiology of her family so that what was most nutritious for them was at the same time what delighted them most. For there is no logical incompatibility between the notions of delight and nourishment.

God cannot be limited by the facts as they are. He need not adjust His choices to the existing particulars nor to those relations between them that we call laws of nature, for by definition He can alter the particulars and the laws as He sees fit. It is said that He is limited by the laws of logic: "There is something God cannot do, namely, make a contradiction true." This is misleading, as suggesting the existence of some kind of possibility that God cannot realize. But logical possibility is simply the broadest notion of possibility there is—unconditional possibility; and it makes no sense to speak of possibilities beyond logical possibility. It is no limitation on the freedom of a traveler that he cannot travel outside space. God can create a planet that is both spherical and composed entirely of the finest steel; He cannot, however, create a planet that is both spherical and cubical. But this does not mean that He can create some kinds of planets and not others. A planet that is both spherical and cubical is not a kind of planet. We do not know what it would be like.

Since theism of the sort we are interested in accepts the first two premises of the argument, our discussion will be concerned wholly with the third:

3. The world is not perfect.

Whoever asserts this claims to know that this world is not the best possible one. The claim is defended by pointing to the evil in the world, noting that it is not logically impossible for there to be instead a world not containing that evil, and concluding that such a world would be a better one. It follows that there are just two ways of rebutting the third premise: (*a*) by denying that there is any evil in this world; or (*b*) by arguing that it is not logically possible for there to be a world containing, on balance, less evil than this one— in other words, all the evils in this world are necessary evils.

The Denial That There Is Evil

SUFFERING and wanton cruelty are examples of what are ordinarily regarded as evils. It may be contended that these are not really evil, if due consideration is paid to their consequences or their parts in the total harmony of things; but this contention will be taken up in the following section. Here we are concerned with (1) the denial that there are any such things as suffering and cruelty, (2) the opinion that although suffering and cruelty exist, they are not evil, even in isolation and apart from consequences, and (3) the contention that "evil" is merely a subjective concept.

(1) *Evil is illusory*. It is conceded that people often think they are suffering; but whenever they think so, they are mistaken.

We might at this point embark on a disquisition concerning the metaphysical distinction between appearance and reality. But I do not think we need to. Suffice it to remark of this view, first, that it is wildly implausible (though this does not prevent it from being affirmed by many people at least in words); second, even if it is granted, it is not to the point. For supposing that no one ever really suffers but only mis-

takenly supposes that he suffers, it nevertheless follows that
the world is *(really* is) such as to contain the appearance of
suffering; and other things being equal, a world not containing that appearance would be a better world. Perhaps it is
better to suppose mistakenly that one is pursued by a green
dragon than to be in fact pursued by a real green dragon;
but it is better still to be neither pursued nor the victim of
a delusion.

(2) *Evil is nonbeing.* When we say that something is bad
or evil, there is an implied reference to a standard which the
thing in question fails to attain. What we really mean (so
goes the argument) is that the thing in question lacks something, is somehow incomplete. But to say that something is
lacking in some respect is not to assign any positive or real
quality to it. St. Augustine said that evil has no efficient cause,
only a deficient cause.[51] Evil, then, considered in itself, is
mere nonbeing, the deprivation of reality, whereas being and
perfection are synonymous. Insofar as anything is real, it is
perfect and good. But everything, except God, is and must be
finite; hence everything, except God, must be evil to some
extent. It is logically impossible that God should create another being not at all evil, for that would be to create another
infinite being, i.e., another God. In summary: evil is nonbeing; but nonbeing does not exist; therefore evil does not
exist.

Like the ontological argument, this one is subtler than it
seems at first glance. To avoid the arduous task of exposing
its metaphysical shortcomings, let us again concede the argument's conclusion and ask only whether it is of any help to
the theist.

It may console the paralytic to be told that paralysis is
mere lack of motility, nothing positive, and that insofar as

[51] *City of God,* ch. 12.

he *is*, he is perfect. It is not clear, however, that this kind of comfort is available to the sufferer from malaria. He will reply that his trouble is not that he lacks anything, but rather that he has too much of something, namely, protozoans of the genus *Plasmodium*. If the theist retorts that evil is nonbeing in the metaphysical, not the crudely material, sense, it would seem appropriate for the victim to inquire why God saw fit that the finitude of His creatures should take just this form rather than some other. Really, the "evil is nonbeing" ploy is a play on words, an unfunny joke. It is a sign of progress, both in philosophical acumen and essential humaneness, that little is heard along these lines nowadays.[52]

(3) *Evil is subjective.* "To god all things are beautiful and good and just," said Heraclitus, "but men have supposed that some are unjust and others just."[53] "Evil" signifies only "that which displeases *us*"; it is cosmic impertinence to reproach the Source of all being for not ministering to all our petty demands. "When the Grand Turk sends a ship to Egypt," the very celebrated dervish asked Dr. Pangloss, "does he concern himself whether the mice on board are comfortable or not?"[54] This would seem to be also the gist of the answer which the Lord spake unto Job out of the whirlwind.

It is apparent, however, that this line of thought is no argument, but rather an injunction to stop arguing. No doubt humility, especially before God, is a fine thing, and doubtless also there are occasions when the best thing to do is to hold one's tongue (to quote the very celebrated dervish again). And I do not wish to deny that the discussions of cosmic evil

[52] This too optimistic sentence was written before I had read Father P. M. Farrell's piece "Evil and Omnipotence" in *Mind*, LXVII (1958).

[53] Fragment 102.

[54] Voltaire, *Candide*, ch. 30.

may afford the chief of such occasions. If we have very good reason to believe that God exists, then certainly this is so. We ought then to accept the existence of evil as a mystery too wonderful for us, and let it go at that. In our investigation so far, however, we have not come upon this very good reason; hence such peremptory silencing is not in order.

In any case, anyone who cleaves to this line must face a serious consequence: he can no longer maintain that God is good. If we grant that the notions of good and evil are devoid of objective validity, that they express the human standpoint only, then if God is not good in this subjective sense (and we would certainly not call a *man* good who deliberately infected his children with spinal meningitis, or conspired to deliver great nations into the governance of criminals), we have no basis for calling Him good in any other sense—for no other sense has any meaning for us. True, we would not call Him evil either—He would be "beyond good and evil." But this fact should be squarely faced. It cannot be the case both that good and evil are terms inapplicable to God and that God is good in any sense of "good" intelligible to us. To demand to have it both ways is not, after all, an expression of humility. Returning to Heraclitus: if the force of "but men suppose that some [things] are unjust and others just" is that these terms "just and unjust" (as well as good and bad, well and ill, and the like) are merely relative to the human point of view, then there is no warrant for the previous assertion that "for god all things are fair and good and just." Or rather, that turns out to be a meaningless sentiment.

Evil Disappears

in the Universal Harmony

BUT perhaps I am unjust to Heraclitus. Very likely what he meant was that men call some things just and others unjust not only because their viewpoint is subjective and biased, but because it is limited; whereas God, who sees the whole of things entire, sees that the whole is perfect and harmonious. In Pope's couplet:

> All Discord, Harmony, not understood;
> All partial Evil, universal Good.[55]

This is the gist of a very popular solution of the problem of evil, one often presented with the aid of analogies from art. Cut up the Mona Lisa into a jigsaw puzzle, and every piece, perhaps, will show nothing but a chaotic mixture of clashing colors. But once all the pieces are fitted together, we see not only that the whole is beautiful but that each "ugly" piece

[55] Alexander Pope, *Essay on Man*, I, 291 f.

makes its indispensable contribution to that beauty. If every piece of the puzzle were itself beautiful, the whole would lack beauty—or at best have the kind of beauty that a quilt may have. Or consider the twenty-fourth measure of the fugue in A minor in Book I of *The Well-Tempered Clavier:* It is

hard to imagine an uglier "piece of music." But of course the point is precisely that this one measure is not in itself a "piece of music"; it has no existence apart from the fugue as a whole; and it would be an idiotic critic who would reproach Bach for not making every individual measure in his fugue melodious. Dissonances, sounded by themselves, are unpleasant, "evil"; but God Himself could not write any extended piece of music, of any worth, that avoided them altogether. May it not be the same with the universe?

It may be—why not? But let us not suppose too hastily that this analogy settles everything. Measures are elements of musical compositions, and human lives are (if you like) elements of the cosmos; but the similitude is rather farfetched. One who hears the whole of the fugue in A minor regards it as a thing of beauty, and he understands how the dissonances necessarily contribute to the beauty of the whole. God, who contemplates the whole cosmos, regards it as a thing of goodness, and He understands how sufferers from inoperable throat cancer, exploders of H-bombs,

> Cattle in the slaughter-pens, laboratory dogs
> Slowly tortured to death, flogged horses,
>   trapped fur-bearers,
> Agonies in the snow, splintering your needle
>   teeth on chill steel . . .[56]

necessarily contribute to the perfection of the whole, which if it did not contain them would be insipid, *ennuyeux.* . . . Or does He? The analogy is getting forced.

The value of the painting, or of the fugue, is to the spectator and to him alone. It makes no sense to ask whether the twenty-fourth measure of the fugue can appreciate the sublimity of the whole. The twenty-fourth measure is not a conscious being and therefore not anything that something might be valuable *to.* It would be silly to say: "Poor twenty-fourth measure! I hope it realizes that its sacrifice is not in vain!" But it would not be silly to say, at the games in the Colosseum, "Poor gladiators! I hope they realize how getting their arms hacked off and their eyes gouged out contribute to the general gaiety of the occasion!" It would be monstrous; and it is a nice question, which is the greater evil: the pain of the combatants or the thrills of the spectators. However that may be, reliance on the analogy of the arts to justify evil seems to attribute to God something like the attitude of Nero.

In brief, the argument under consideration is this: just as a work of art, which as a whole possesses high aesthetic value, must contain elements that considered in themselves lack

[56] From "The King of Beasts," by Robinson Jeffers; copyright 1948 by Robinson Jeffers; reprinted from *The Double Axe and Other Poems*, by Robinson Jeffers, by permission of Random House, Inc.

aesthetic value, or even possess disvalue, so also the universe, which as a whole is the best possible, must contain elements (e.g., the sufferings of sentient creatures) which considered in isolation would be evil. The objection to the argument is that values are realized only in sentient experience, from which it follows that when some whole has sentient beings as elements, we can speak of the value of that whole in at least two different senses: as the "sum" (admittedly, in a vague sense) of all the values, positive and negative, experienced by the elements; or as the value that is experienced by a sentient spectator who contemplates that whole. In the first sense, the value of the whole cannot be a maximum unless the value in the experience of each element is maximal; suffering always diminishes the total value. In the second sense, while the value experienced by the spectator may be (in psychological fact) increased by disvalues experienced by the elements, this can be so only if the spectator is callous or sadistic. Either way, the conclusion is the same: the aesthetic analogy affords no way out of the problem of evil.

Evil Exists

for the Sake of Greater Good

THE argument just criticized tried to show that the evils in the world may be necessary elements in a pattern which is as a whole perfect, though the elements if considered by themselves would have to be regarded as more or less evil. That is, perfection is a quality of the whole that does not appertain to the individual parts; nor do those parts contribute to the perfection of the whole in any other way than by fitting into the pattern. In short, the qualities of the individual parts are irrelevant to the quality of the whole.

Although the argument that we will now take up is frequently confused with this aesthetic argument, it differs in that it conceives the goodness of the universe as composed additively of the goodnesses of the parts. Therefore any evil in the parts detracts from the good of the whole. Nevertheless, it is insisted, the whole is as good as it possibly can be. "Best of all possible worlds" does not mean "world with no evil in it"; it means "world with the greatest possible excess of good over evil." And our world, we are assured, is the latter world.

If all the evil were miraculously eliminated from the world, a great portion of the good would go with it, and what remained would be so insipid that we would yearn to go back to the "bad" old days. This not on account of perversity, but because many goods are such that they cannot exist unless some evil exists also. On the merely sensuous level, it is great delight to slake one's thirst with a tall cool drink on a hot day; but there would not be, and could not be, any pleasure in a tall cool drink if no one were ever thirsty. But thirst, by itself, is unpleasant, "evil." If the value (i.e., pleasure) of slaking thirst is assigned 5 "hedonic units," and the disvalue of being thirsty has -3 units, then the complex being-thirsty-and-drinking has a net positive value of 2 units. Therefore a universe containing thirst-and-slaking is better than one containing neither; and the universe must contain both or neither.

On a more elevated plane: the most justifiable ground for human pride and self-congratulation lies in man's conquest of nature, his use of intelligence to make two ears of corn grow where one grew before, to stamp out beri-beri, to sail the seas and fly through the air. Now no doubt God could have played the overindulgent father and made Iowa full of hybrid corn, neatly planted in rows and weeded, to greet the first settler; made human beings immune to all disease; provided bridges across all the oceans, and given men feathery wings. In that case, however, men would have suffered the common fate of children whose parents spoil them: they would all be lazy, ignorant, and good for nothing. On a higher level still: God could have arranged things so that no one ever suffered, but if He had, the virtues of compassion and charity, or indeed moral virtue in general, could not have existed.

In order to state this argument with somewhat more precision, let us distinguish two classes of goods and evils, which we shall call primary and secondary. The primary goods (what some writers call "natural" goods) are pleasures and enjoyments. Secondary goods (or moral goods, or virtues) are the dispositions of conscious, purposive beings to produce primary goods, especially in others. Similarly we define primary evils and secondary evils (vices). Eating when one is hungry is a primary good. The disposition manifested in setting up a soup kitchen for the down-and-out is a secondary good. Being horribly mangled is a primary evil. Instigating a war is a secondary evil.

We now have to account for the existence of both primary and secondary evils, on the ground that their existence is necessary to bring about greater goods than could be actualized in their absence.

We can see right off, as in the example of thirst, that some primary evils must exist if some primary goods are to exist; and if our considered judgment of the matter is that we would rather have both the evil and the good than neither, then we have no ground for complaint—unless we see fit to protest that God could have arranged things so that necessary primary evils were always followed by their correlative goods, as He has not. (Thirst is not always quenched.) In the example of intelligence (which I treat as a primary good, or intensifier or abettor of primary goods, though of course it enters into secondary goods as well), the relation is more complex. It is strained to justify the affliction of millions of men for countless centuries by beri-beri, on the ground that some medical men and chemists were thus afforded the opportunity of tracing the cause of the disease to vitamin B deficiency. It has been observed, however, that one of the principal sources of primary evils, as well as goods, is the uniformity of nature. God could have made nature nonuniform, so that unwary individuals stepping over the edges of precipices were "miraculously" wafted back; but it appears that such a nonuniform nature would offer little scope or opportunity for the exercise of intelligence. Intelligence would be unnecessary if all our needs were taken care of; and hopelessly lost if there were no discernible patterns. There is point in Pope's rhetorical query:

Shall gravitation cease, if you go by?[57]

One might question why so many of the uniformities of nature must be uniformly disastrous in their consequences for sentient creatures; but we should admit that we are not really in a position to judge. It is best to concede the possibility that primary evils—even the enormous totality of suffering involved in the evolutionary process—must exist to produce the greatest surplus of primary good. (I do not find this plausible, but that may be owing to a personal blind spot.)

In any event, it would seem that a better (or at any rate supplementary) justification for primary evils can be afforded in terms of secondary goods. Secondary goods are parasitic on primary evils: no charity without poverty, no heroism without distress, no patience without annoyance. Let us concede also that secondary goods, which are the peculiar goods of character, are transcendently more important than primary goods, so that it is meaningless to attempt a quantitative comparison of the primary and secondary. That is, let us concede that any amount, however great, of primary evil is more than offset by any amount, however small, of secondary good. Then a world, such as ours, which does contain secondary goods must both contain primary evil and be better than any world not containing primary evil. And since we cannot pretend to know how much primary evil is necessary to afford proper scope for how much secondary good, we must allow the possibility that God has permitted only the minimum

[57] *Op. cit.*

amount of primary evil to exist. Thus far, then, it may be the case after all that this is the best of all possible worlds.

One consequence should be noted before we go on: if we take advantage of this reasoning, it follows that God's goodness is not secondary goodness, as ours is, but is what we should have to call "tertiary," a disposition to maximize secondary goodness. God's goodness, that is, does not lie (primarily, at any rate) in His disposition to alleviate suffering and promote enjoyment—He is not kind and sympathetic in the human sense; rather, His goodness has as its object the promotion of kindness, sympathy, etc., in *us*. This is, of course, no objection. Tertiary goodness is a recognizable kind of goodness even in human beings, e.g., in parents who concern themselves with developing the characters of their children. It is not always just cruelty that leads parents to deprive their children of various comforts and even to inflict positive pain on them "for their own good."

There is, however, an insuperable obstacle to accepting this reasoning as a satisfactory rebuttal to the argument from evil: to wit, the existence of secondary evil. Notoriously, human beings are not all and not always kind, sympathetic, and courageous; they are also malicious, selfish, and cowardly. If it is God's purpose to maximize secondary goodness in His creatures, He has obviously not done so; and since there does not seem to be any way of showing a log 1 impossibility in the maximization, by an omnipotent Being, of that goodness, it looks as if the argument in justification has collapsed. True, there are some varieties of secondary goodness—such as courageous resistance to tyranny, or "turning the other cheek" —that presuppose secondary evils. But it would be a grotesque stretching of the limits of rational concession to allow that all the secondary evil in the world must exist for the sake of these particular secondary goods.

Free Will

THE objection that we have just offered, based on the existence of moral evil, is the target for the most powerful weapon in the theist's armory: that of free will.

Of course (it is said) God could have made all men perfectly "virtuous," into beings that never committed any wickedness, never thought any impure thoughts, etc. But this conception of "virtue" is spurious. Men of this sort would be mere automata, marionettes, with God as the Great Puppeteer. They would utterly lack responsibility for their acts. And lacking responsibility, they would be no fit objects for praise or blame. Such "virtue" as they exhibited would be imposed from outside; it would not be *theirs;* they would not be moral agents at all. The only goodness in the universe, then, would be primary goodness, enjoyed by these zombies—as we have already seen, a relatively insignificant kind of goodness; plus the goodness (now only secondary) of God. The creatures would not have real secondary goodness, which must come from within; nor would God Himself have any tertiary goodness. Such a universe would obviously not be the best possible, if instead the omnipotent Being, Himself a moral agent, could have created other moral agents.

And of course (so the argument goes) He has actually done so: God has endowed men with free will and real moral responsibility for their acts.

What does it mean to be a moral agent? A moral agent is one who can, and does, make real choices, all by himself. He is confronted with situations in which there are two or more lines of action that he can pursue—*really* can: nothing outside himself predetermines his choice. Here is the path of virtue, there is the path of vice. If you go one way—not pushed— you are virtuous, a fit object of moral praise; if you take the low road, you are vicious, and it is well to denounce you and punish you.

But if finite beings are to be real moral agents in this sense, not only must they be able to choose the wrong alternative, but it is a necessary consequence of their being free that sometimes they will choose wrongly. Hence freedom, which is the greatest good, as well as a presupposition of real secondary goodness, necessitates the existence of secondary evil. But freedom is such a great good that it is worth whatever price must be paid in secondary evils. And men, not God, set the price; for moral evil is their doing, not God's. If cruelty and all kinds of depravity are rife in the world, men should reproach their fellows, not God.

Let us set this argument out in systematic form:

1. Moral goodness (secondary goodness, virtue) is qualitatively superior to natural goodness (mere enjoyment). A world not containing moral goodness could not be the best of all possible worlds.

2. Moral goodness is possible only to moral agents.

3. A moral agent is a sentient, intelligent person who is capable of making, and at least sometimes does make, real choices.

4. A real choice is one the outcome of which is not pre-determined by any factor outside the agent, i.e., not within his control.

5. Responsibility for a real choice lies solely with the agent.

6. It is logically possible for there to exist moral agents besides God.

7. Hence (from 1, 2, 3, 6, and the definition of God) if God exists, He has created moral agents.

8. Men are moral agents.

9. Therefore (by 3, 4, and 8) men sometimes make choices not predetermined by God.

10. If men's choices are not predetermined by God, He is not morally responsible for them.

11. Moreover, if it is always possible for men to choose wrongly, they will sometimes actually make wrong choices.

12. Hence (from 5, 9, 10, and 11) there is moral evil in the world, but it is the responsibility of men, not of God.

13. Therefore (by 1 and 12) the existence of any amount of moral evil is compatible with this world's being the best of all possible worlds, and with the existence of God.

If all the premises of this argument are true, then the argument from evil is destroyed, or at least very severely scotched. Let us look at some of them.

The crucial premises are 1, 4, and 11. The first is conceded. We shall begin our examination with the fourth.

Real Choices

4. *A real choice is one the outcome of which is not pre-determined by any factor outside the agent.* But the choice *is* determined by the agent; it is not merely capricious.

This definition might be taken as an arbitrary one, in which case asking whether it is true would be pointless. Since, how-ever, this premise in conjunction with premises 3 and 8 entails the conclusion that there are real choices as here defined, we might as well consider right now whether we are prepared to admit the probability, or even possibility, that anything actually corresponds with this definition. (The question is not whether there are any real choices, in some sense: of course there are.)

Premise 4 is a sweeping one: it entails that both determinism and predestination are false. Since the incompatibility with predestination is obvious, I shall discuss only determinism.

Determinism is the doctrine that the principle that every event has a cause, holds without exception. If determinism is true, then no action by a human being is an exception, and there can be no real choices in the sense of premise 4. For then my every act of choosing has a cause. The cause may not be any factor outside myself, to be sure; we might be inclined to say that the cause of my choice is my motive, where this vague term apparently stands for some sort of psychological set toward the alternatives. This set may or may not be analyzable ultimately in terms of my physiology, especially the state of electrical and chemical activity in my nervous system; that does not matter. The point is that while the immediate cause of my choice may be no factor outside myself, this immediate cause is a link in a causal chain stretching indefinitely outside me in space and in time. I may have ice cream or pie for dessert; I choose ice cream. Why? Because I like ice cream better. Why? I do not know in detail; but if determinism is true, the explanation consists in principle of some combination of statements describing my inherited dispositions (heredity) and what has happened to me since I was born (environment). This does not mean that I cannot alter my environment, but it does mean that an environment, unaltered by me (because I was not yet born), got in the first licks, so that what I subsequently do to my environment is determined by (causally explicable in terms of) what my environment first did to me. In this respect I am no different from a bomb which goes off and destroys a city. The immediate cause of the explosion is in the fuse, internal to the bomb; but nobody supposes that the explosion is on that account "the bomb's fault." Everything that happens is explained in terms of what went on outside the bomb, and before there was a bomb.

And it goes without saying that I had nothing to do with my heredity, and cannot alter it.

Philosophers debate whether determinism ought to be understood as a very sweeping hypothesis, or as a presupposition for the application of scientific method, or as a resolution not to give up the search for causes, or what not. This again is a problem we need not pause to consider. If it is a hypothesis, then at least conceivably it is false with respect to some acts of human beings; and the evidence for its truth, while considerable, is mostly indirect and not by any means conclusive. If determinism is a presupposition or a resolution, there is no law that says *we* have to presuppose it or resolve it in our present context. In other words there is no veto on our rejecting determinism, as the fourth premise solicits us to do. We are free to work out the consequences of discarding it, and for all we know our conclusions may correspond with reality.

A consequence of the assumption that determinism is false is that some deliberate actions of human beings either have no causes at all, or if they do, the causes form only short causal chains that do not proceed outside the scope of the individual's sovereignty. These acts, and these alone, are real choices. Since they are actions independent of external factors, they afford just the occasions for saying truly that the chooser could have chosen otherwise than as he did. Some person, X, is confronted with alternatives A and B. He chooses A. But in exactly the same conditions there would have been no physical impossibility about his choosing B instead; or at least, if there had been, the choice of B would have been impossible simply as a result of conditions internal to X, so that if one traced X's biography back far enough, one would come to a point where independently of the rest of the universe he made some choices that proved ultimately incompatible with B.

Let us give a concrete illustration of what this indeterminist doctrine claims. A brilliant student—let us call him Raskolnikov—is on the point of having to discontinue his studies for lack of funds. The opportunity arises to obtain money by murdering and robbing an old pawnbroker. Raskolnikov decides, after considerable conscious reflection, to do the deed, and he does it. He is not acting under anybody's order or suggestions, nor in order to please anyone else; it is strictly his own idea. Now of course the state of the universe, especially of his immediate circumstances, was not irrelevant to the decision; for instance, if he had been rich he would not have done it, or even thought of doing it. Nevertheless this sort of action springs from a real choice, if there is any such thing as a real choice. He alone was responsible for it, we say; he could have helped it; he could have refrained from doing it.

All this is true, according to the present doctrine; and what it means is that the spring of the action was internal to Raskolnikov. No doubt his genetic make-up and his circumstances disposed him to the act, made it a real temptation; but the temptation was resistible. At some point in the proceedings—perhaps an instant before he picked up the ax, perhaps many years before—something *he* did, something moreover that he could have refrained from doing even if everything else had been the same, made it inevitable that he would split the old woman's skull. Whatever the decisive factor was, it was not something out of his control, not some accident of environment or fortuitous concourse of genes.

And that is why (the indeterminist story goes on) we do right to hold Raskolnikov responsible, why we rightly say he was legally and morally guilty, and why Raskolnikov himself acknowledges the justice of these verdicts. On the other hand, if determinism were true, then he could not have helped it; and people are not responsible for what they cannot help doing. He could not have helped it, because on the determinist hypothesis, given Raskolnikov's heredity, and given everything that had happened up to the moment of so-called decision, only one outcome was possible. He could no more have helped picking up the ax and bringing the sharp edge down on the old woman's head than the typewriter on which this is being written can help spelling out CAT when I depress first the C, then the A, then the T. True, Raskolnikov "deliberated," i.e., thought the matter over, and "struggled with his conscience"; but that whole process would be, in deterministic terms, only more complex than the motions of the levers and linkages in the typewriter, not different in kind. One step would succeed another inevitably; and anyone who knew in detail all about Raskolnikov's heredity and environment could predict with certainty what he would do. If only he made his calculations fast enough, he could even tell Raskolnikov what he was going to "decide" before he "decided." Obviously in such a case the "choice" would be utterly spurious.

Well, is determinism true, or is it not? Obviously we cannot decide the matter by a crucial experiment. We would have to observe someone making a choice in a given set of circumstances, then we would have to repeat those circumstances *exactly*. If the subject chose A the first time, and B the next, then we would know that determinism is false. But of course we can never set up the experiment. We cannot repeat a set of circumstances exactly, because something very relevant and upsetting, namely the subject's memory of the previous occasion, is bound to be different in the second instance.

But (the indeterminist concludes his case) determinism, as we have seen, makes nonsense of the notions of guilt and responsibility, which are indispensable to morals. Hence if there are reasons why scientists must assume that determinism is true, there are equally compelling reasons why moralists—and plain men—must assume that it is false, at least with regard to the deliberate actions of men.

Now let the determinist have his say:

Either the decision to commit the murder had a cause or it had none. If it had no cause, was not the outcome of anything else at all, whether internal or external, then it was completely a chance occurrence—something over which neither Raskolnikov nor anyone else had any control—and would be even less an action for which responsibility could be imputed than what people do when they black out. We like to think of ourselves as masters of our fates, captains of our souls; nothing could be more disturbing than the possibility that next minute or next year we may find ourselves doing something that is in no way traceable to what we are now: something that we have no intention of doing, something that fills us with horror to think of. But if some human actions have no causes, then this fear must become a very real one. Well, perhaps we *do* do such things; if we do, though, we should certainly protest, and rightly, that we ought not to be held responsible for them. So we see that an act that has no cause cannot possibly, in any sense, be a real choice.

To be sure, the indeterminist does not maintain that the decision to commit the murder had no cause at all; only that the cause, or the crucial factor in the total cause, was internal in the sense described. But that (says the determinist) does not help matters. If the cause was a part of a short chain that began in Raskolnikov and was not linked to anything outside, then the same considerations apply to the beginning of that chain. If it had no cause, then a fortiori Raskolnikov did not cause it. Only that which has a cause can be controlled. If one is helpless before externally caused events, one is even more helpless before utterly fortuitous ones. If you cannot help doing what your heredity and environment "make" you do, neither can you help doing what you just *find* yourself doing. Hence if determinism makes nonsense of responsibility. indeterminism does so even more thoroughly.

And anyway (the determinist continues) it is simply not true that determinism is incompatible with responsibility. For what is a choice—a "real" choice if you will? It is just a kind of interior process of thinking about the probable consequences of the alternatives open; getting clear, if one can, about which is morally right and which wrong—in short, totting up the reasons for and against, and coming to some sort of resolution. The fact that choice is caused does not mean that the process of choosing is nonexistent. Nor does the possibility that a person with enough information about us might predict our decision mean that there is anything bogus about choosing. We take pride in being dependable, reliable, *predictable* in our behavior, especially our rational deliberate behavior.

But do we not *know* that we can confound any prediction, if we want to? Perhaps I always ask for ice cream; but if someone says, "I know what you're going to do before you do it," I shall order pie instead, just to show him I can! And is this not enough to refute determinism?

By no means. If someone predicts my behavior, he must do it on the basis of information he already has. He may have complete information; if so, he should be able to predict with certainty. But now, if he makes his prediction, *and tells me what it is*, this itself alters the initial conditions of my act. True, he can take account of this, and make a new prediction; but if he tells me about that one, again I can confound him at will. I can always keep one jump ahead of him. There is nothing in this that is incompatible with determinism; nor is there anything about it that ought to be degrading or frightening. Probably what most people are afraid of, when told that all their doings are caused, is that somehow an inexorable fate is making them do what they do not want to do; but if determinism has anything to say on this score, it is that you *must* do what you want to do, not that you cannot.

What, moreover, is the point of blaming people and punishing them for their wrong choices? Presumably, it is to discourage them and others from doing likewise in future—to alter their behavior patterns, *cause* change. This is, or may be, an efficacious procedure if determinism is true; just as far as determinism is false, so far also is it futile to try, by causal means—and we have no other means—to "reform" or intimidate anyone. We do not punish the insane, nor do we punish sane people for what they do accidentally. Why not? Just because punishment can be a deterrent only in relation to deliberate actions; it will have no effect on the insane person, who cannot deliberate, or on those who do wrong without previous intent. We punish some kinds of negligence, but only in order to insure that undesirable behavior, which was not deliberate this time, will be thought about in advance next time. But perhaps punishment is vengeance, and it is not right to take vengeance on one who (in the determinist sense) could not help doing what he did? So much the better! Vengeance is a relic of savagery. Determinism helps to bring this out (and for that matter, so does indeterminism).

It is not an abandonment of his doctrine for the determinist to tell someone that he could have helped doing what he did. The point of the reproach is not that, given your circumstances and motives on the past occasion, these were just as compatible with the opposite decision as with the one you made; rather, it is that when you acted you were capable of giving due consideration to elements of the situation that you neglected and that you are well advised to do so in similar future situations. "Raskolnikov, you could have let the old woman alone" means something like "Raskolnikov, you are now and were then a rational being, that is, one capable of being influenced by moral considerations, and of imaginatively picturing to yourself the deplorable consequences of ax murders. You didn't control yourself on that occasion, but next time pray do, and apply instead for a student loan." It does not mean: "It was just a toss-up what you would do"; and if it did mean that, then the question of moral responsibility simply would not arise.

A Middle Way: Self-Determination?

The preceding discussion is a sketchy presentation of one of the most vexing of philosophy's perennial problems. Perhaps the reader suspects that the indeterminist's side has not been fairly presented: that what he holds is not that real choices have no cause, but that they are *self*-caused, where "cause" has a sense different from what it has in the sort of billiard-ball model case assumed: That is, real choices flow from the person's character, and character is not altogether the mere resultant of external buffetings—and even when it is, one can always make the effort to reform.

I confess inability to make any sense of this suggestion that is different from the determinist interpretation of it (i.e., we can reform our characters if we want to; but wanting to is, like everything else, caused). But that does not matter. Let us assume, for the sake of argument, that there is some sense in which character is crucially independent of external circumstances, and that real choices are choices that are expressions of character. It is easy to show that this assumption does not lead to any consequence different from indeterminism as previously described. For in this case I am responsible for what is an expression of my character: "real choice" means "choice that is an expression of my character." Some people have vicious characters, others have virtuous ones. But how is this difference to be accounted for? By hypothesis, not completely in terms of heredity and environment. Then how? You are responsible for your act, because it flows from your character; but it will not do to say that you are responsible for your character, because it flows from your character. All we can say is that A has a virtuous character, and B has a vicious one, and that is the end of the matter. It is just a piece of luck, in the purest and most distressing sense, who has which. "But you make your own character." Who is this *you*? Is he characterless? If so, how can he be a determinant of one type of character as against another? Does he have some character already? Then how is its distinctive nature to be accounted for? Either luck or regress *in infinitum*.

If we are to avoid luck on the one hand and the sloughing off of ultimate responsibility on the other, it seems we must struggle to form the conception of a moral agent who is what he is neither for no reason at all nor for any reason depending on something else being what it is. That is, the moral agent required would have to be "cause of itself." I confess I do not know what this means; but whatever it may mean, if anything, metaphysicians and theologians who use the term are unanimous that it applies only to God. And indeed it is obvious, on both physical and theological grounds, that no human being is cause of himself. Therefore at best there can be only one moral agent meeting the specification; in which case premise 6 is false.

Now let us see what has been established so far:

Either all human actions are part of a determinist pattern, or they are not. If they are determined, then the fourth premise ("A real choice is one the outcome of which is not predetermined by any factor outside the agent") is false; or, if you prefer, vacuous. Although in that case there remain senses of "real choice" and "moral responsibility" that make these terms useful and (generally speaking) applicable to the cases in which we in fact do apply them, still in the last analysis what any man does is the resultant of his heredity and environment. God, if omnipotent, made the heredity and environment, or at any rate consented to them; and, if omniscient, He foresaw what would result from them; thus God is the ultimate cause of everything everybody does. If He had willed it to be otherwise, it would have been otherwise. Hence moral evil is the result of God's will. But it is logically possible for there to be a world in which there would be no moral evil, or at least not nearly so much; and such a world would be better than this one. Therefore this is not the best of all possible worlds, hence God (with a capital *G*) does not exist.

On the other hand, if not all human actions are determined, then some are undetermined or self-determined. If some undetermined actions are crucial to cases of moral importance, two consequences follow. First, God could have made them determined, and such as to embody moral goodness, thereby avoiding moral evil. Second, although God Himself logically could not foresee the characteristics of undetermined actions, and therefore could not prevent their occurrence, no human being could do any better; so that if God is not responsible for them, neither are men. Moreover, we are invited to imagine the unedifying spectacle of God throwing dice with human souls: "Let's see how *this* one turns out."

Last, if the crucial human actions are self-determined, that is, flow from the agent's character, then this character either is what it is for no reason, and we are back with indeterminism; or if there is some reason why it is what it is, this reason must be, ultimately, that God willed it to be that way instead of some other, and we are back with determinism.

The upshot is that there is no intelligible way to make out a case for refusing to impute moral evil to God; hence the attempt to refute the argument from evil by an appeal to human free will is a failure.

If the considerations advanced in support of this conclusion are not convincing, the free-will defense still fails in premise 11:

11. *Moreover, if it is always possible for men to choose wrongly, they will sometimes actually make wrong choices.*

This premise is a particular instance of the "principle" that what is always possible is sometimes actual—a doctrine devoid of both logical and factual support.

The doctrine is not a principle of logic. If it were, we could use it to prove the actual existence of anything conceivable, including God. Unicorns, fairies, and men a thousand miles tall are all logically possible; but there never have been and never will be any such creatures. Nor is it a principle of fact. We may understand "factually possible" in at least two senses. In the first sense, only that is factually possible which is compatible with the laws of nature and with the past history of the universe. In this sense, to be sure, the factually possible is identical with the sum, past, present, and future of what exists. But this trivializes the "principle" into the linguistic stipulation that "factually possible" is to be taken as synonymous with "actual at some time," and premise 11 becomes, "if men sometimes sin, then they sometimes sin"— which is useless for the argument.

The other and more usual sense of "factually possible" is "not incompatible with the laws of nature." In this acceptation we say that it is possible for John Smith to work harder than he does, or that it is possible (as far as we know) for the sun to explode tomorrow. But then, in this meaning of the term, clearly many things are possible that are never actual.

In spite of this, the "principle" has an appeal that has led many subtle thinkers to accept it: for example, St. Thomas Aquinas in the Third Way: "That which is possible not to be, then some time is not."[58] Probably what lies in the back of their minds is the thought that in the fullness of time every possible combination of things will turn up. That may be so; but it is important to note that the "things" that are to enter into all possible combinations must last long enough, so that at best this speculation could apply only to the fundamental and unchanging units or atoms of the cosmos (if there are any such things). And men are not fundamental and unchanging units of the cosmos.

It is possible that someone might stand on his head and recite the Constitution backwards immediately after being inaugurated President of the United States. But even if our institutions endure to eternity, there is no guarantee that anyone will ever thus amuse the citizenry. If the unit of our speculations be taken as the life of one individual, it is even more evident that any one man realizes only an infinitesimal fraction of the possibilities open to him.

The point need not be labored further. Premise 11 is just not true. The true statement that is confused with premise

[58] *Op. cit.* (see note 29).

11, and that lends it whatever plausibility it has, is this: if all men are *prone* to choose wrongly, they will sometimes actually make wrong choices. But to make men so that it is possible for them to sin, and to make them prone to sin, are quite different things.

For consider the saints. A saint is a man who never sins— or who sins so seldom and venially as to make no practical difference. But it is just as possible for a saint to sin as for anyone else; the difference is that the saint is not prone to sin. And if, as is admitted, God has made some men saints, it cannot be logically or factually impossible for Him to have made all men saints. If He withheld this grace in the vast majority of cases, then He has not created a world containing the irreducible minimum of moral evil, hence has not created the best of all possible worlds.

In conclusion, let us consider the suggestion that the evils of this world are made up for in the next. We can be brief about this, for it should be clear by now that this affords no way out. No doubt it is a good thing for finite, clumsy mortals to offer reparation for the damage they do; but it is not seemly to apply the analogy to a perfect Being. It is better, even for men, not to do any damage in the first place. It is said that evil exists in order to test men's characters. That is nothing to the point. An omniscient Being would have no need of such tests, unless characters were throws of cosmic dice. Besides, such tests could have no point other than as a basis for assignments to eternal bliss or its opposite. If all souls go to Heaven, as the Pelagian heretics maintained, then the tests would be purposeless: why set examinations for your students if you have decided in advance to award all of them highest honors? I shall not pursue the other alternative, of an infinitely benevolent Being who consigns some of His creatures to unending torture.

Conclusions

OF course there may be some vitiating error in the argumentation of this part. But if not, then not only is it the case that, in Hume's words, "Epicurus' old questions are yet unanswered," but no answer to them is possible.

There cannot exist, compatibly with this world, a Being who is at once omnipotent, omniscient, and benevolent, where benevolence is taken in a sense intelligible to men. I do not pretend that anything in this part is incompatible with the view that the goodness of God is beyond (I will not say above) reason, a mystery that must remain unfathomable by mortals. We shall consider later the contention that if reason leads to such and such a conclusion, then so much the worse for reason. But an exhortation to abandon reason is not a reason for believing anything.

Part IV

PRAGMATISM

Review and Transition

IT is well to pause and recall what question we are trying to answer in this book, and to consider what progress we have made toward answering it.

The question is, "Is it reasonable to believe that there is a god?" The question is not just, "Is there a god?" The difference between these questions needs to be emphasized. From the mere fact that a statement is true it does not follow that anyone who believes it is being reasonable; nor does the mere fact that it is false make all belief in it unreasonable. Take the statement "Base metals can be transmuted into gold." This happens to be true, yet it was unreasonable for medieval alchemists to believe it, because all the evidence available to them was to the contrary. The establishment of a theory of chemical elements in the eighteenth and nineteenth centuries made it if anything a more unreasonable belief. A belief is reasonable if what is believed accords with the evidence available at the time; and in a different though related sense of "reason," one is unreasonable who expects a man to anticipate evidence that in the nature of the case cannot be acquired until the process of inquiry has been systematically advanced much further. (In the present example, knowledge of atomic structure is the evidence needed.) This is not to say that it was unreasonable for alchemists to entertain the hypothesis that new facts, bearing on the other side of the question, might be discovered; nor even that it was unreasonable for them to busy themselves in the search for such facts. All that was unreasonable was the belief that certainly there existed a solution to their problem.

Or consider the statement that the earth is the fixed and absolute center of the universe. This is false, but it was not an unreasonable belief for the ancients to have held. It squares with the ordinary appearances of things, which were all they had to go on.

Last, take the sentence "There are more than two but less than three tons of gold in the cubic mile nearest the north pole of the planet Venus." Since there now exists no evidence at all, direct or indirect, bearing on this statement, neither believing it nor disbelieving it is reasonable. The rational attitude is suspense of judgment.

We can distinguish three kinds of degrees of reasonable belief. The first and highest is belief based on sound inference from all the relevant evidence there is or can be, the believer knowing that he is aware of all the evidence. To say that a proposition is rationally credible in this sense, and to say that it is true, amount to the same thing. But this is the God's-eye view of things; one may doubt whether any human being ever has attained it, or could attain it, with respect to any matter of fact less obvious than that the cat is on the mat. We cannot pay serious attention to any claim that some individual has arrived at it in the realm of belief we are discussing.

The second degree of rational credibility, perhaps the highest for men, pertains to beliefs based on sound inferences from all the evidence known to anyone at the time, and thought to be relevant.

The third degree of reasonableness is relative to a given individual, who bases his degree of assent on inferences, made as judiciously as he can, from evidence known to him.

The three degrees of rational credibility, then, are all relative: the first, relative to God (or, if you prefer, Absolute, or Truth with the capital *T*); the second, relative to the highest development of knowledge achieved by humanity; the third, relative to the knowledge of the individual.

If much is at stake, an obligation devolves on the individual to make his belief jibe with the second degree; he ought to revise his belief in accordance with information available but not yet actually acquired by him: he can consult an expert, or look it up in the encyclopedia. The experts themselves have a professional duty to increase humanity's sum of knowledge. Dogmatism consists in confusing either the second or third degree with the first.

Now to return to our question. If we had put it flatly, "Is there a god?" the appropriate answer would be in terms of the first degree of rational credibility, and we would be asking, in effect, "Does God know that there is a god?" As human beings, however, we must limit our aspirations—which may be arrogant enough—to achievement of the second degree.

In this book so far, therefore, we have been inquiring whether it is reasonable to believe that there is a god, where "there is a god" is taken to be a statement of alleged fact (like "there are neutrinos") and the criteria of reasonableness are cogency of inference and attention to all available evidence. That at any rate has been the aim. Bearing in mind the stipulations of usage for "deity" and "God," we can summarize the conclusions so far reached:

The Existence of God

1. *It is not reasonable to believe that God exists.* For it is reasonable to infer that if God exists, then this is the best of all possible worlds; but the available evidence does not support this conclusion.

2. *It is not reasonable to believe that there is a deity.* For there is no reason to think it certain or even probable that anyone has perceived the existence of such a being; and all the indirect arguments which purport to establish his existence are unsound.

3. *It is not unreasonable to entertain the hypothesis that there is a deity.* Not just on the tenuous grounds that all reasoning is fallible—on those grounds it would be reasonable to entertain the hypothesis that the earth is flat; but more positively, because the existence of a deity, although not a hypothesis that is required to explain any known fact, is also not logically incompatible with any known fact.

These conclusions need not shock anyone. What they boil down to is this: it is the God of Greek philosophy, not of popular religion, that is ruled out. For all we have said, it is still possible for there to exist a personal cosmic force, very powerful, very knowing, and very benevolent. Although I do not want to involve myself in sectarian doctrinal controversy, I cannot forbear remarking that as far as I know there is nothing in Holy Scripture that asserts, either directly or by clear implication, the existence of God; only of a very august deity. Such a personage might be, if you like, infinite or perfect in as many as two of these respects. (I find it hard to understand how a being might be perfect in two of these ways and not in the third; but no doubt I am lapsing into the thought pattern of the cosmological argument.) The circumstance that all the arguments fail which attempt to prove the reality of such a being, may be interpreted as showing that these modes of proof are simply inappropriate in this context;

because the existence of a deity, if it is to be called a fact at all, is a fact of a unique kind.

With these conclusions, and with this comfort, if it is a comfort, we should be finished with the question of the reasonableness of belief in a god, and I could end this book, were it not that "reasonable" has other senses besides those so far considered. We speak not only of reasonable beliefs but of reasonable men; and the reasonableness of men does not consist entirely in their proportioning assent according to the weight of evidence. Men may succeed brilliantly in thinking rationally, yet fail miserably to act reasonably. Let us consider further this notion of reasonable action.

I suppose it will do to say, rather roughly and vaguely, that reasonable action is expedient action. We all have lives (and perhaps afterlives) to get through, and reasonable action is what we can do, by our own deliberate efforts, to make the best of things. Nearly everybody would agree that some things are more worthwhile than others, and I suppose there is general agreement that health is better than sickness, knowledge is better than ignorance, awareness better than torpor, serenity better than anxiety, creativity better than destructiveness, love better than hatred. A man's life is a good one, a happy one, insofar as he manages to realize in it a surplus of these values, and of others. Expedient or reasonable action, then, is action that is intended to, and does, produce a good life—whether for the agent himself, or for others; I do not want to say that self-sacrifice is inexpedient or unreasonable. But self-sacrifice *is* unreasonable unless *some* good is likely to come of it.

Given the particular circumstances of an individual human life, however, it is seldom or never possible to maximize all the varieties of value. Not just because ours is an age of specialization, but because in the nature of things intense creativity may in some individuals be cultivated only at the expense of health; love may demand sacrifice of serenity; etc. Nor does it seem possible or desirable to draw up general rules of precedence to enable us to tell, by consulting them, that a value high on the list is worth the sacrifice, total or partial, of one lower down.

Now reasonableness, taken in the sense used hitherto in this book, is certainly a value, a desirable ingredient of the good life. But it is not the only value there is. We must investigate its relation to some other values.

(With apologies, and merely to avoid tedious repetition of distinctions, I shall hereafter sometimes use the expression "scientific outlook" instead of, and as synonymous with, "reasonableness" in the sense employed in Parts I–IV; "science" instead of "reason," and "scientific belief" for the previous "reasonable (or rational) belief." And when referring to conduct, I shall use "expedient" as synonymous with "reasonable." I wish I could think of a less tendentious set of near-synonyms, but I cannot; and I prefer not to coin a jargon of my own. While we are on the subject of terminology, the reader is also hereby put on notice that I shall hereinafter use "Deity," with capital *D* and capitalization of pronouns, to mean what, in accordance with the definitions laid down in the Introduction, would be described as an august deity, such as is recognized by the major monotheistic religions still current. I beg any theologians who may be reading this to indulge me and not insist that only what I have previously referred to as capital-*G* God satisfies this definition.)

It will be granted that knowledge is valuable for its own sake, that it is worthwhile to know just for the sake of knowing, even when no parsnips are buttered. We should not say in all cases that a man was a fool who gave up health or wealth just in order to satisfy his curiosity. And science, being the most reliable means of acquiring knowledge, at least in a very wide area, partakes of this value.

Yet knowledge, like anything else, can be bought at too high a price. It may not be expedient to let the victim of leukemia know what ails him. Man's knowledge of nuclear physics is disastrous. And the scientific outlook can lead to absurdity: what should we say of a husband who, returning from the wars, declared that since he had no evidence one way or the other concerning his wife's faithfulness, he was suspending judgment pending a report from a reliable firm of detectives?

In general, though, it is expedient to be scientific. For in order to get what we want, we need to know the pertinent facts and the relations that hold among them. The scientific outlook may be viewed as the outcome thus far of the evolutionary adaptive process. It differs, however, from most other manifestations of that process in being not a merely passive adjustment of organism to environment, but rather in making possible the reverse adjustment of environment to organism. The bear must go over the mountain to see what he can see; but if man is annoyed at having his view obstructed, he can abolish the mountain.

In sum: science is worthwhile for its own sake, regardless of consequences.

> It fortifies my soul to know
> That though I perish, Truth is so.[59]

But the principal value of science is as an instrument for keeping us from perishing and for facilitating the achievement of other kinds of value. Science is, moreover, a multipurpose tool. In a community of angels, no doubt it would be an un-

[59] Arthur Clough, "With Whom Is No Variableness," quoted by William James in "The Will to Believe" (see note 71, below).

alloyed blessing. But with men as they are, possession of certain kinds of knowledge may conceivably lead to the destruction of every value, including science itself. Hence it is not *always* expedient to be scientific; or, to lapse into our previous terminology, it is not always reasonable (in the sense of furthering values in general) to be reasonable (in acquiring and systematizing information). The probability that if all men were always reasonable in both senses, there would be no conflict, does not alter the case. For it is not reasonable, in either sense, to ignore the existence of unreason.

Furthermore, science at best has value as an instrument only in those situations in which there is objective control of belief. Let me explain what I mean. Adopting the plausible view that a statement is true when it corresponds with reality and false otherwise, we can say that a true belief is belief in a true statement and a false belief is belief in a false statement.[60] The practical advantage of having true beliefs rather than false ones is that true beliefs do not get you into trouble, whereas false ones do. A belief may be regarded as an anticipation of experience, on the basis of which one works out one's strategy. If the situation turns out to be as foreseen, i.e., if one has true beliefs about it, then the strategy will work; otherwise not (except by luck). I believe that the XYZ Corporation is going to quintuple its sales in the next year. On the basis of this belief, I invest my scholar's mite in XYZ stock. If the belief is true, all is well; if not, I am shirtless. In other words, beliefs—however acquired and maintained, whether products of the scientific outlook or not—find their test, their control, in confrontation with objective reality. The instrumental value of

---

[60] This is to be taken as a stipulated definition. I agree with Austin that "it may be doubted whether the expression 'a true belief' is at all common outside philosophy and theology" (J. L. Austin, "Truth," in *Philosophical Papers* [Oxford: Clarendon Press, 1961], p. 86).

the scientific outlook derives entirely from the fact that beliefs formed in accordance with it have a greater chance, on the whole, of passing the objective test—of "working"—than beliefs that result from wishful thinking, superstition, etc. On the whole, one likes to suppose, people who invest on the basis of economic knowledge make more profit than those who consult fortunetellers or stick pins at random in the financial page.

There are two classes of beliefs, however, to which these considerations do not apply. I shall call one class self-confirming beliefs and the other uncontrolled beliefs.

I may believe, for any reason or none, that the XYZ Corporation is going to fail. On the basis of this belief, I sell all my XYZ stock at once. If I own enough stock, this action of mine may bring about the condition that I anticipated; though perhaps if I had not sold the stock, the corporation would have prospered. Governor Faubus believed that if Negro students were allowed to attend Central High School, there would be violence. The very announcement of this belief made it probable that his belief would be confirmed. We need to note carefully, however, that what is confirmed in these instances is not the original belief, if that belief is taken to be about what will happen in any case even if the believer *does* nothing. Governor Faubus's original belief may well have been false; we shall never know. But there is nothing unscientific about anyone, including Governor Faubus, believing that if a high public official makes dire predictions of violence, then it is likely that there will be violence.

Uncontrolled beliefs fall into three classes: those that are in fact never tested by the believer, though they might be; those that are never tested by anyone, though conceivably they might be; and those that are logically incapable of being tested.

I may believe that sharks can be scared away by shouting and splashing. This belief may be true; if false, it still may comfort me when I make an ocean voyage. If I do not have the misfortune to fall overboard in shark-infested waters, the belief is not put to the test and I come out ahead, having been spared the anxiety of worrying about what to do in that situation. And of course the whole point of a belief may be to make people take precautions so that it is not put to the test. The belief that one is likely to get cramps if one swims immediately after eating is false, I am told. But most people refrain from swimming after eating, hence do not test the belief. (I am not advising anyone to test it.)

No one has prospected the north pole of Venus for gold, and perhaps no one ever will. Hence if it should fortify anyone's soul to believe that that land abounds in gold, the facts will not confound him.

Beliefs that for logical reasons cannot be tested at all fall into two categories: those for which no factual test conditions can even be imagined by anyone; and those rendered impervious to test because the believer refuses to interpret any event as telling against them. As an example of the first, we might take metempsychosis: the belief that has been held by very many people, including Plato, that at bodily death the soul does not perish but goes to animate some other creature. Since the trauma of birth is said to destroy all memories, and there is no other conceivable way of telling whether or not the present soul of this hippopotamus used to be the soul of that philosopher, such a belief, if held, cannot possibly come into conflict with any fact. The second category is illustrated by delusions of persecution. The paranoiac believes that everyone is conspiring against him; overtly hostile behavior is taken as confirmation, while kindness is "seen through" as a disguise intended to put the victim off his guard. Any behavior whatsoever of other persons can thus be accommodated to the persecution hypothesis. (Reverse paranoia, the inexpugnable belief that everybody loves one, does not occur, so far as I know. Or perhaps when it does, the modification of personality is not unpleasant, so that it does not come to the attention of psychiatrists.)

Let us call all these kinds of beliefs, which are either not tested or untestable, "overbeliefs." Of the kinds of overbeliefs just enumerated, let us assume that there are at least some in each category that are significant, i.e., true or false. (This is clearly the case with respect to the first two kinds.) It seems probable that the vast majority of any person's beliefs are overbeliefs, mostly of the first kind. Now the drawback to holding false beliefs that are, or are likely to be, put to the test is the surprise, danger, and frustration resulting when reality knocks them down. But how can this objection apply to overbeliefs? Does not expediency dictate a policy of holding overbeliefs that are most comfortable, that lead to peace of mind, amiability, and confidence? Or in other words, are not the overbeliefs that lead to satisfactory adjustment to reality—the great advantage of true, tested beliefs—just the ones that make one happy? In short, don't they *work*?

It occurs to one immediately that such a policy would not be expedient, in general, with respect to overbeliefs of the first class: those that while not actually tested may be tested. This is so for two reasons. First, we cannot be sure what situations we may eventually find ourselves in—after all, I may fall into shark-infested waters some day. It is to my advantage to be prepared and have a true belief, right now, about how to scare sharks. Second, if I do not personally test these beliefs, others will, and I shall hear about it, and unless I am willing to give up faith in the general reliability of testimony (and that would put me at a great disadvantage in coping with reality) I shall not, as a matter of psychological fact, be able to retain just those that are comfortable.

These objections apply only with much-diminished force to overbeliefs of the second kind. About all that can be said is that it would be a bad, inexpedient habit to get into, to make up one's mind about the inaccessible regions of the universe on the grounds of what is most pleasing, because of the danger that the habit would infect one's attitude to matters of practical moment. But in any case, overbeliefs of the second kind are rather rare and not of much importance, as was suggested by our example.

It is with the third kind that the question becomes most serious. And it is right in this area that we encounter most of the typical dogmas of religion. If someone believes that there is a Deity, or that his soul is immortal, or that virtue and vice are always appropriately recompensed in the afterlife, he may be confident that he will never run into any circumstances in which as a result of these beliefs he will be surprised, or frustrated, or put in danger. Moreover, those who hold these beliefs assure us that life would not be worth living if they had to give them up; their effect here and now is the enormously important one of facilitating adjustment to reality. Is it not, then, obviously expedient for us to hold to these overbeliefs if we have them, to try to acquire them if we do not have them, and to adopt those social arrangements that encourage their acceptance and discourage their questioning or rejection?

This line of thought is the pragmatic argument: even if we have no scientific reason to believe that there is a Deity, it is nonetheless reasonable, i.e. expedient, to believe that there is, because the belief "works."

This argument is very old, and exists in several versions, which differ one from the other mainly in the kind of "working" that is emphasized: whether the happiness of the individual, the welfare of society, or the furtherance of morals. I venture to say that it is the most powerful and influential of current theistic arguments, although it is seldom stated quite frankly in public. Or rather, *because* it is seldom stated. This last remark brings us to an important point about the pragmatic argument, one that we would do well to appreciate before we begin our scrutiny.

The point is this. If the pragmatic argument is advanced as the *only* support of religion, then just insofar as this is generally understood, to that extent religion must be undermined. So that to be effective the pragmatic argument must, on account of pragmatic considerations, be kept among the esoteric doctrines. Let me illustrate with an analogy.

A parents' discussion group may soberly debate the question whether it is a good thing to encourage their children to believe in Santa Claus. They may come to the conclusion, most judiciously and reasonably, that it is. The belief tends to make children both happy and good; and the bad effects, if there are any, are outweighed by the desirable ones. The parents may then resolve to encourage the belief for the benefit of all concerned.

But if the children overhear the discussion, all is lost. And not just because of childish resentment at being duped. The children might even understand their parents' viewpoint and accept their arguments. It is just that believing in Santa Claus, and believing that it is a good thing to believe in Santa Claus, are quite different, and to convince someone that it is a good thing to believe in Santa Claus, and that this reason is the only one for believing in Santa Claus, is an infallible way of getting him *not* to believe in Santa Claus. This is not to deny the obvious fact that the cause of someone's believing P can be, and very often is, no more than that P is pleasant to him.

But once this fact is permitted to penetrate to consciousness, and the subject is convinced that his alleged reasons for believing P are all spurious, then there is no more belief in P. Beliefs have got to be rationalized—though the rationalization may be no more than a hazy feeling that "everybody believes P," or "you've got to have faith," or even be quite inarticulate. To believe P, and to believe that P corresponds with reality and that moreover there is some sort of respectable reason for believing P, even if the believer has not got the foggiest notion of what it might be—all these are the very same thing. And the mere pleasantness of P does not count as a reason—not even to those most prone to wishful thinking. To be sure, someone may say, and mean it: "If I could no longer believe in P, I couldn't go on living." And the person may in consequence be inaccessible to considerations urged as objections to P. But the very fact of this resistance to criticism is proof, if any is needed, of the point being made: for it shows that "after all, it is pleasant to believe P" is not a last, inexpugnable line of defense for belief in P; it is no defense at all.

That is why the pragmatic argument is of no force to convert the infidel and why theists do well to enunciate it *sotto voce.* Ordinarily it is combined with other arguments and appeals; if it were not, just stating it might be disastrous to religion. But of course if I am convinced on other grounds that there is a Deity, then it does no harm to point out that believing in a Deity has good consequences.

One more word, before we begin a more systematic discussion of the argument. The concern of this book is solely with the question of reasonableness of belief in the existence of a god, and the pragmatic argument will be discussed as if it were simply an attempt to show the reasonableness of believing in a god. This does not quite do justice to the argument, since it is ordinarily not used for the specific purpose of defending belief in the Deity but as a general defense of "religion." For example, the official piety of the American government seems to be based on the doctrine that only religious persons can be good citizens and sufficiently anti-Communist. This is one version of the pragmatic argument. That is why United States consuls inquire of prospective immigrants whether they believe in God. But I doubt whether a pious Jain, or Theravada Buddhist, would be excluded solely for answering the question negatively—at least not if he appealed to more sophisticated echelons in the State Department. Religion, any religion, is enough. We are a tolerant people.

The Pragmatic Truth Argument

PRAGMATIC arguments in support of theism are of two general sorts: those that attempt only to show that it is expedient to believe in a Deity and those that claim to show that because the belief is expedient it is *true*. The latter kind of argument is both newer and more complex than the former; nevertheless I shall examine it first. For this purpose I shall provisionally concede that belief in a Deity is expedient: that individuals who possess this belief are happier, more creative, more sociable, more vital, and so forth, than agnostics and atheists; also that societies in which belief is widespread have the advantage—any kind of advantage you like—over irreligious cultures and nations.

The kind of argument we are now to consider is identified with William James, whose originality and importance as a philosopher of religion cannot be overestimated. James, like most innovators, had scant respect for the tradition he inherited; nowhere is this more evident than in his treatment of rational theology. In the lecture entitled "Philosophy" in his *Varieties of Religious Experience*, he briefly summarizes some of the material that we have treated in Part II, not concealing his impatience with the subject: "I will not weary you by pursuing these metaphysical determinations farther" is a typical remark. He says finally: "In all sad sincerity I think we must conclude that the attempt to demonstrate by purely intellectual processes the truth of the deliverances of direct religious experience is absolutely hopeless." His very next sentence, however, is even more revelatory of his attitude: "It would be unfair to philosophy, however, to leave her under this negative sentence." One might have thought that if the arguments were no good, it was religion that was left under a negative sentence. But no: if philosophy does not prove that religion is true, so much the worse for philosophy, not for religion. He goes on to suggest that the philosophy of religion should transform itself into the empirical study of the common essence of the great religions.

Elsewhere, though, we learn that James's philosophy *can* prove that religion is true. The argument, in outline, is very simple:

1. It is expedient to believe that there is a Deity.
2. But expedient belief is identical with true belief.
3. Therefore belief in a Deity is true belief.

The argument is set out most completely in "The Sentiment of Rationality" (written 1879–1880),[61] a paper the very title of which is a résumé of James's argumentative strategy.

Since the first premise is provisionally conceded, we need to discuss only the identification of expedient belief with true belief.

The statement is, on its face, outrageous; yet James makes out an astonishingly persuasive case in its favor. The version I shall now present is not a summary of any single passage in

[61] In *The Will to Believe, and Other Essays in Popular Philosophy* (New York: Longmans, Green, 1912).

James's writings, and here and there it may touch on points not dwelt on, or even mentioned, by him. It is intended, though, to be a fair outline of the reasoning whereby truth is identified with expediency.

The first move is to relegate to the attic of metaphysics the correspondence theory of truth—to get rid of the notion that "truth" means the property that a proposition has when it corresponds with reality and lacks when it does not. The trouble with this definition (according to James) is that it is useless. No doubt God directly perceives ultimate reality and can immediately and finally check any proposition against it. We are in no such position. All we have to go on is our experience, and such indications and hints as we may glean from it. As was suggested before, of the three degrees of reasonableness, the second is the highest attainable by man, who therefore cannot legitimately concern himself with anything higher. The correspondence view of truth, however, appertains only to the God's-eye view. For that reason we should abandon it. No one is ever in a position to claim that he knows something nontrivial to be true in that sense. Let us then cast off these arrogant pretensions and focus our attention on the second degree, and let us signalize our abandonment by defining "truth" in humanly significant terms. We shall, then, want to say that our beliefs are true when they accord with all the available evidence.

So far, so good. We may at least provisionally accept this redefinition, unless we balk at the consequence that the very same belief could then be true today on the evidence at hand and false tomorrow when new evidence turns up. It would sound strange to say, "It's false now that the earth is flat, though it was true in the seventh century B.C." But why not say this? All it comes to, if we remember the new definition, is the innocent and unexceptionable assertion that we are now aware of evidence for the sphericity of the earth that was not available in the seventh century B.C. If we claim to be "nearer the truth" than our ancestors, we can support the claim only by citing evidence that we have but they did not have; and just the merit of the revised definition is that this fact is brought out into the light. The alternative "absolutist" conception of truth suggests that over and above knowing that we now possess extra evidence, we know also (and this knowledge is distinct from knowing the extra evidence) that we are nearer the absolute ultimate truth of things, to the God's-eye view. But since we never see anything from this superhuman vantage point—and if we did, we would not know that we did—there can be no sense, either, in saying that now we are closer to it.

One more qualification, or perhaps I should say elucidation, is needed before the proposed definition can be accepted. We do sometimes say, "All the available evidence is in favor of P, yet I still don't know whether P is true or not"; and the definition, as I have stated it, would make such statements absurd. What we need to add to the definition, "true" = "according with all the available evidence," is some further stipulation such as "the quantity of evidence being sufficient to establish it beyond reasonable doubt." Admittedly this is vague, but that is the fault of the human situation. What is enough evidence cannot be determined by rote application of rules. Nevertheless juries when they convict, and scientists when they decide to stop calling some statement a hypothesis or theory and to start calling it a law, do manage somehow to estimate how much evidence is enough. Our business here is not to inquire into the details of the process. Clearly it is a rational one, if there is any such thing as a rational process.

Roughly: when the jury foreman announces, "We find the defendant guilty of murder in the first degree," he and his peers are *doing* something—perhaps depriving someone of his life—and doing it on the basis of a belief that the evidence so preponderates in favor of guilt that it justifies an action of the last degree of seriousness. The scientist is in effect saying that the hypothesis is so well supported that to seek further confirmations would be a waste of effort. Thus finding a statement true amounts to doing two things: deciding that the evidence now preponderates in its favor and predicting that no more evidence, or at least not enough more to upset the balance, will be discovered. Due recognition should be given that such predictions always can go wrong and often do; but that is hardly reason for refusing to predict at all, to become an utter skeptic.

The first step, then, in the pragmatic argument is this redefinition of "truth" as "according with the evidence, etc." We have been taking it for granted that we know well enough what is meant by "according with the evidence." But we need now to make this more explicit. Otherwise we may lapse into conceiving of "*the* evidence" as something wholly or partly "out there," wholly or partly independent of our experience; and we would be no better off than we were with the correspondence theory. We need to explain "evidence" in terms of experience and to explain what is to be understood by "according" with it.

Before we can do this, however, there is a prior question to resolve. At present we can say this: what we believe, when we believe anything, is that some statement is true, i.e., accords with the evidence. But what is a statement? Marks on paper, vibrations in the air? These are not the objects of our beliefs; more accurately, what we believe to be true is what the statement conveys, its meaning. But let us not be tempted to ask, at this point, What is meaning? It is more fruitful to ask, What kind of process is "grasping the meaning of a statement"?

The pragmatic answer to this question was set out by Charles Sanders Peirce in his 1879 paper "How to Make Our Ideas Clear."[62] To grasp the meaning of a statement is just to know what it would be like for the statement to be true. If my young son asks me what "solubility" means, I will tell him that it is the property, which some things have, of dissolving in liquids. If that is not sufficient, I will say something like this: " 'Sugar is soluble in water.' What this means is that if you take a lump of sugar and put it into a glass of water and stir the water, after a while there will be no more visible white lump; yet the sugar is still there, as you can tell from the sweet taste of the water." The statement "marble is soluble" is false; nevertheless its meaning is similarly elucidated, as what it would be like for marble to disintegrate and become invisible if stirred in water.

We can generalize from these examples. To ask what a statement means is to ask what it would be like if the statement were true; and this in turn is to ask what would result if certain conditions were satisfied, or in other words, what would *happen* if we *did* so-and-so. The directions for getting at the meaning of a statement, then, are these: first transform it into a conditional (if-then) statement, in which the if clause describes something you might *do* and the then clause describes the experience you would have in that case. "What you might do" refers to what it is logically possible for you to do, not what you have the inclination, ingenuity, time, power, money, etc., to do. Thus "There are green men on

[62] First published in *Popular Science Monthly;* reprinted in *Collected Papers,* V (Cambridge, Mass.: Harvard University Press, 1934), and in numerous anthologies.

Mars" means "If you were conveyed to Mars (never mind how), you would see beings with the general shape of human beings, but green in color."

Peirce drew two consequences from this analysis. The first was that two statements that differ verbally have nevertheless the same meaning if their possible consequences in experience are the same. Take "Smith is a civil servant in the State Department." Roughly, and in part, this means: "If I apply for a passport, I shall be referred to Smith, who will ask me to fill out forms, pay a fee, etc." Now take "Smith is a bureaucrat in the State Department." The consequences in experience are exactly the same, so the two statements have the same meaning, hence "civil servant" means the same thing as "bureaucrat."[63] Peirce, of course, was concerned only with cognitive meaning; the two statements differ in signifying, or producing, different emotional reactions, hence differ in "emotive meaning." But one might expect different treatment— to be subjected to more fussiness, more red tape, less courtesy—from a bureaucrat than from a civil servant. In that case, the two terms are not cognitively synonymous for the individual who has these different expectations.

The second consequence was that if it makes no conceivable difference in experience whether a given statement is true or not, then the statement in question has no cognitive meaning. One of Peirce's examples concerns the doctrine of transubstantiation: "In the most holy sacrament of the Eucharist, there takes place a wonderful and singular conversion of the whole substance of the bread into the body, and of the whole substance of the wine into the blood, of our Lord Jesus Christ, the species of bread and wine alone remaining."[64] Catholics

[63] The example is not Peirce's.

[64] Decree of the Council of Trent (1551); quoted in *The Church*

assert this, Protestants deny it. But according to Peirce, neither party is really believing or disbelieving anything, since the possible effects on experience of a change in substance (which is by definition not seen, heard, tasted), not accompanied by a change in sensible properties, is nil.

It is easy to see what a powerful engine this analysis creates for demolishing various "metaphysical" beliefs. It would seem also that much or all of theology must go if we accept the doctrine; and in fact many philosophers, convinced by Peirce, have rejected theology as meaningless.

But not William James. He gave Peirce's pragmatism a new and ingenious twist—much to Peirce's annoyance. The twist consisted in accepting this account of meaning—that the meaning of a statement is the difference its truth would make in experience—while broadening the notion of experience so as to include not just sense experience, as Peirce had intended, but anything at all in the life of the individual. Let us see how James did this and what the consequence was for his religious philosophy.

Peirce had intended his pragmatism to supply only a method for getting at the cognitive meaning of statements. As far as truth was concerned, he retained an orthodox view. In "The Fixation of Belief," a companion piece to "How to Make Our Ideas Clear," he wrote that the "fundamental hypothesis" of the scientific method, which he contrasted favorably with other methods, religious and metaphysical, for settling doubts, is this:

There are Real things, whose characters are entirely independent of our opinions about them; those Reals affect our senses according to regular laws, and, though our sensations are as different as

Teaches, by Jesuit Fathers of St. Mary's College (St. Louis: B. Herder, 1955), p. 286.

are our relations to the objects, yet, by taking advantage of the laws of perception, we can ascertain by reasoning how things really and truly are; and any man, if he have sufficient experience and he reason enough about it, will be led to the one True conclusion.[65]

Yet in the same essay Peirce insists that "the settlement of opinion is the sole end of inquiry"—including scientific inquiry; "inquiry" is defined as "a struggle to attain a state of belief," and we are told that the reason why we so struggle is that doubt is irritating.

James exploited the tension in Peirce's philosophy between, on the one hand, the view that the object of inquiry is to get at the truth and, on the other, the insistence that inquiry is over whenever the irritation of doubt is alleviated. If the meaning of a statement is the difference its truth would make in experience, then (James reasoned) belief in a statement is belief that my experience will be as described; and the truth, of statement and belief alike, lies simply in my experiences being as anticipated. To believe, then, is to wager that one will not be let down when in the context of the experiences that constitute the meaning of the belief. To believe falsely is to let oneself in for the shock of surprise at least, for disaster at worst. So if one is never surprised, never discommoded, this is the test, and the only test, of the truth of one's belief. To say that a belief accords with the available evidence is just to say, then, that experience never imposes on us any penalty for holding that belief. This leads at once to the famous pragmatic definitions of "truth": "An Idea is 'true' so long as to believe it is profitable to our lives,"[66] and *"The 'true' . . . is only the*

[65] First published in *Popular Science Monthly*, 1877; reprinted in *Collected Papers*.

[66] "What Pragmatism Means," in *Pragmatism* (New York: Longmans, Green, 1907), p. 75.

expedient in the way of our thinking . . . in the long run and on the whole of course."[67] Briefly, true beliefs are beliefs that "work."

There are no restrictions or qualifications on these definitions. To say that true beliefs are beliefs that "work" would be innocent enough, and platitudinous, if one were talking only about kinds of beliefs that are always in imminent danger of breaking down because they have to do directly with external reality and are put to the test all the time. The beliefs that potatoes are nourishing and that fire burns, work; beliefs that arsenic is healthful and that your banker will not make a big fuss about a tiny overdraft do not work. To be sure, James renders obeisance to the "logical demand": one way for beliefs not to "work" is by their being inconsistent with other beliefs. Thus belief that $247 \times 17,409 = 4,300,021$ does not work, even if no one ever has occasion to multiply these numbers, because it is inconsistent with a lot of other beliefs that are tested all the time, such as that $7 \times 9 = 63$. But if a certain belief is such as to be always expedient, always profitable to our lives, no matter what happens or could happen, then that belief is true, and that is the end of it.

James takes as basic the notion of belief, as a kind of psychological "set," rather than the notion of meaning. The Peircian criterion of meaning is thrown overboard—or, to speak more politely, modified. Peirce's criterion of meaning, it will be recalled, is this: to get at the meaning of a statement, ask yourself, What would I have to do to put it to a test? And what would the perceived consequences be if it were true (in the orthodox sense of "true")? James asks only: What are the consequences in experience—*any* experience, not just a test-experience—of your belief? If they are profitable—"in the long run and on the whole of course"—then the belief, the psycho-

[67] "The Notion of Truth," in *ibid.*, p. 222.

logical set, is true and the question of meaning does not (or need not) even arise.

Application to Religious Belief

It is obvious how these doctrines may be applied to belief in the existence of a Deity. The question whether this belief is true reduces to the question whether it is reasonable; and the reasonableness of the belief is identical with its profitability or expediency, which in turn can be decided only by surveying the consequences of holding the belief. If belief in a Deity is inconsistent with some other profitable belief, then one or the other will have to give way. But fortunately it does not clash with any other important profitable belief, as is shown by the impossibility of proving that there is *not* a Deity. What we might call direct settlement of the question—actual confrontation with the Deity—will come, if at all, in afterlife, and we are concerned here only with what can be confirmed or invalidated in our mundane experience. And there is the peculiarity that even if the belief turns out, after death, to be "false," the believer would never know it, never be surprised or shocked, except in the unlikely eventuality—unlikely for James, though not for some Buddhists—that immortality and atheism are both true. Therefore the only consequences in experience that are pertinent to deciding whether the belief is true are the effects the belief has on the believer. These, we have conceded *arguendo*, are profitable. Therefore there is a Deity.

The Pragmatist's Dilemma

As far as I can see, there is nothing logically defective in all this, and I have no wish, for the present, to dispute any of the premises. Yet, considered as an argument whose aim is to make one believe in a Deity, it is obviously a failure. Why?

If I accept the premises and the reasoning, I come out with

the conclusion that there is a Deity, *in the pragmatic sense.* But this is an extraordinarily Pickwickian sense. In virtue of the definitions, it reduces to the belief that belief in a Deity is comforting. But this belief is not the comforting belief!

If when on safari through darkest Africa I contract some hideous tropical malignancy, I may observe that thè natives who get it recover when they submit to the dosages and incantations of the local witch doctor. They really do recover, and those not so treated really do die in agonies. The reasonable, even the scientific thing for me to do, then, is to call in the witch doctor. But when I do, he tells me that he can do nothing for me unless I believe *(really* believe) that he is supernaturally endowed with the powers of the great spirit Mumbo Jumbo. So I am doomed after all. No matter how I try, I cannot bring myself—even to save my life!—to believe in the existence and magical efficacy of Mumbo Jumbo and his agent. I believe that if I believed, all would be well; that is, I believe that belief in Mumbo Jumbo is expedient. Nor is it unreasonable to jettison science and everything else when survival is at stake. But that is not enough. All I can do is try to fortify my soul by knowing that though I perish, Truth is so. A pragmatist philosopher in the situation would be no better off. The belief that is efficacious from the pragmatic point of view must be a belief not in the pragmatic "truth" of Mumbo Jumbo's existence but in the old-fashioned, "out-there" reality of that benevolent deity.

Let us compare, in this context, the famous argument in favor of theism—specifically, in favor of Roman Catholicism—known as "Pascal's Wager."[68] The pious mathematical genius Blaise Pascal anticipated the pragmatists in considering beliefs as bets. To believe, or disbelieve, in God is in effect to bet that He exists or does not exist. Very well, then, if I am to

[68] Blaise Pascal, *Pensées*, Pt. II, sec. 2, 3.

bet on a rational basis, I had better consider the odds. What is there to win or lose? If I believe (bet) that God exists and He does ("out there"), I win eternal bliss; if I bet on His existence and am wrong, I lose nothing of any consequence. On the other hand, if in betting against His existence I prove correct, I have gained nothing either; whereas if I am wrong in this wager, I am damned for eternity. Consequently I have everything to gain and nothing to lose in betting that God exists; and that is therefore the rational thing to do.

Pascal of course overlooked the fact, which James and others pointed out, that the betting situation is not so simple; for many religions, incompatible with Roman Catholicism, offer the same odds. But he was very much aware that to be convinced of the expediency of betting on God was not the same as holding the beliefs necessary to salvation. What then is to be done? Pascal was frank:

You would like to attain faith, and do not know the way; you would like to cure yourself of unbelief, and ask the remedy for it. Learn of those who have been bound like you, and who now stake all their possessions. These are people who know the way which you would follow, and who are cured of an ill of which you would be cured. Follow the way by which they began; by acting as if they believed, taking the holy water, having masses said, etc. Even this will naturally make you believe, and deaden your acuteness [*vous abêtira*].⁶⁹

Nor was James, perhaps the greatest psychologist America has yet produced, unaware of this crucial difficulty. And he was not content with the rather naive *Looking-Glass* technique suggested by Pascal.

"I ca'n't believe *that!*" said Alice.

"Ca'n't you?" the Queen said in a pitying tone. "Try again: draw a long breath, and shut your eyes."

⁶⁹ *Ibid.*, quoted by James in "The Will to Believe."

Alice laughed. "There's no use trying," she said: "one *ca'n't* believe impossible things."

"I daresay you haven't had much practice," said the Queen. "When I was your age, I always did it for half-an-hour a day. Why, sometimes I've believed as many as six impossible things before breakfast."[70]

There is no way, James thinks, to produce in oneself a belief *ex nihilo*. Practically, however, most Americans have some tendency to be theists; and it is possible to cultivate the propensity in one, and to shield oneself from the winds of doctrine. James, in his most celebrated essay in religious philosophy, tells us how.

[70] Lewis Carroll, *Through the Looking-Glass*, ch. 5.

The Will to Believe

THE burden of James's paper "The Will to Believe"[71] is that there is nothing intellectually disreputable about maintaining a pre-existing religious belief, or in encouraging a tendency to believe, in the face of the rationalist objection that such belief is devoid of support from evidence.

The "religious hypothesis" according to James is (in part) this: "The best things are the more eternal things, the overlapping things, the things in the universe that throw the last stone, so to speak, and say the final word. 'Perfection is eternal.'" James argues, first, that if this hypothesis cannot be scientifically verified, neither can the principles of induction and causality, which are the foundations of the scientific method itself; so that the antireligious rationalist cannot support his claim to superiority over the believer in respect of not believing without evidence. The second consideration James offers is the complex and subtle argument which at-

[71] First published in *New World*, 1896; reprinted in *The Will to Believe* (New York: Longmans, Green, 1912) and in numerous anthologies. All quotations in this section are from this essay, unless otherwise indicated.

tempts to show that the rule of not believing anything unsupported by evidence is an irrational rule.

This argument has nothing to do with the peculiar pragmatic conception of truth. On the contrary, James evidently assumes in the ordinary way that the statement "There is a Deity" (or rather, "Perfection is eternal") is either true or false. He also assumes, for the sake of argument, that there is no evidence, in the ordinary sense, for or against this; or if there is, then it is evenly balanced on a knife edge. What then is the rational thing to *do* about the religious hypothesis? Believe it, disbelieve it, or withhold judgment?

The rationalist (we are told) cannot countenance believing it in the absence of evidence. By the same consideration, he cannot counsel outright disbelief. Suspense of judgment, then, is the reasonable attitude. But is it? The really reasonable maxim concerning beliefs is that we should believe truth and avoid error, each of these being equally important. But avoiding error, by suspending judgment, is not the same as believing truth; so a policy of refusing to believe except on the ground of adequate evidence may assure success at avoiding error, but only at the expense of missing certain truths, if some of the beliefs thus shunned happen to be true. Nothing ventured, nothing gained.

In certain kinds of cases, to be sure, it is wise not to commit oneself in the absence or insufficiency of evidence. These are the cases where it does not matter much what we believe —the cases, in other words, in which we are not called upon to act. Is there a Himalayan Snowman? Are there antineutrinos? It makes little difference to me whether there are or not; or even to those who investigate such hypotheses professionally. They may get emotionally involved in the issues, but they do not have to. The options of believing, or disbelieving, in Himalayan Snowmen and antineutrinos are what James calls "avoidable options." It is important to note that they are avoidable even for the investigators, who can carry out their searches and experiments without committing themselves in advance to any views about the probable outcomes.

Some options, however, are *forced*, not avoidable: we *have* to take a stand, for suspending judgment amounts in practice to the same thing as adopting the negative. This is where the pragmatism comes into the argument. If my house is on fire, and there is no evidence as to whether or not my children are in the upper story, then if I say, "I suspend judgment about this matter, and shall wait for more evidence to settle it," the effect is the same as if I had decided that the children were not there; and if the children happen to be there, then they will be roasted just as surely if their father is a skeptic as if he were a dogmatic unbeliever.

Besides being classed as forced or avoidable, options may also be momentous (as in the last example) or trivial (Is tomorrow Aunt Agatha's birthday? I must either send her a greeting card, or not; but she sets no great store on such observances, and anyway it's clear that I have no hope of being mentioned in her will); and lastly, *living*, when there is some tendency to believe (Are there or have there been intelligent creatures on Mars?), otherwise dead (Are there English-speaking donkeys on Mars?). All these contrasts, and especially the last, are relative to the individual: what is a living option for one man may be dead for another. If one has already quite firmly made up one's mind that theism is true, then the argument of James is superfluous; if one has decided, with equal firmness, that theism is false, then it is of no avail. James's audience is composed of persons who are to some extent favorably disposed toward theism—who think it possible that there is a Deity and think also that it would be a good thing if there were one—but who "have doubts" and do not know what to say to critics.

A *genuine* option is one that is forced, living, and momentous (e.g., the option of believing, or disbelieving, that my children are in the burning house; Harry Truman vis-à-vis the belief that dropping atomic bombs on Japan would shorten the war). With respect to these, James defends the thesis that

our passional nature not only lawfully may, but must, decide an option between propositions, whenever it is a genuine option that cannot by its nature be decided on intellectual grounds; for to say, under such circumstances, "Do not decide, but leave the question open," is itself a passional decision,—just like deciding yes or no, —and is attended with the same risk of losing the truth.

The application to religion is easy to see. The option of believing or disbelieving in a Deity is forced—we *must* make Pascal's Wager, one way or the other; momentous—if there is a Deity, this is, in its consequences for us all, incomparably the most important fact there is; and living, at any rate for most of us. Living, we are sometimes assured, even for those who reject it altogether at the conscious level: "There are no atheists in foxholes." In this case, then, as in the case of any genuine option not intellectually decidable, we do, as a matter of fact, let our passional nature decide; to put it more bluntly, we believe what we want to believe. The novelty of James's position is that he does not deplore our deciding thus as a departure from rationality to which mankind is lamentably prone, but boldly asserts that we "lawfully may" do so, i.e., it is reasonable to believe what we want to believe. For what is the alternative? It is suspense of judgment; in action that is indistinguishable from disbelieving. But *a rule of thinking which would absolutely prevent me from acknowledging certain kinds of truth if those kinds of truth were really there, would be an irrational rule.*

To put it another way: of the propositions whose truth cannot be decided on intellectual grounds, some presumably are true and some false. But the policy of taking no chances would result in one's always losing the truth of those among the undecidable propositions that were true. Although we might thus be sure of avoiding error, we would be equally sure of not getting the advantage of some momentous truths. If undecidable propositions are as likely to be true as false, then if we picked which ones to believe by eeny-meeny-miney-mo, we would be no worse off than the rationalist. But if we add the momentous consideration that in the case of religious belief the consequences here and now of believing are profitable,[72] then it is clear that religious skepticism, which amounts the believer, who is unreasonable.

Criticism

This argument is vitiated by failure to distinguish *believing what is true* from *knowing the truth*, and by a confusion of *believing* with *deciding what to do*.

Long ago Plato pointed out that one may get from Athens to Larissa by following a guide who knows the way, or by setting out, tossing a coin at each crossroads, and by sheer luck stumbling into Larissa at last. In either case, the result is the same: one has arrived at Larissa. But we should not on that account say that the coin-tosser knew the road. Guessing right is not the same as knowing; nobody before James ever suggested that it was. We may agree that "*we must know to disbelief, is not the rational policy. It is the skeptic, not the truth; and we must avoid error . . .* are our first and

---

[72] This is the "second part" of "the religious hypothesis."

great commandments as would-be knowers"; but it does not follow that when an option between propositions is not decidable "on intellectual grounds" (i.e., not decidable at all—what other *grounds* for decision about *truth* could there be?), then guessing counts as knowing. This is not a verbal quibble; for what the sincere believer wants to say is that he *knows* there is a Deity, i.e., not only is it true that there is a Deity but also that he has reasons to believe it—or at least that someone whom he trusts is believed to have such reasons. Once we distinguish between believing and guessing, then at most James has shown only that the theist has a right to say to his critic, "Well, in religion all is guesswork, and my guess is as good as yours." But to take this attitude is certainly not to be devout, any more than to believe that religious belief is expedient is to have religious convictions. In fact, the argument of "The Will to Believe" is only the pragmatic "truth" argument with the doctrine of pragmatic truth replaced by the confounding of knowing with guessing. This confusion, however, is less defensible intellectually than the straightforward redefinition of "truth."

The appeal of "The Will to Believe" is largely based on James's insistence that there often arise circumstances in which it would be foolish, or worse, to refuse to act because we lack sufficient evidence of what is the best course to take. We may grant that such situations are the rule, not the exception. This kind of consideration is only relevant to questions of belief, though, if belief is identified with tendency to act. And such identification is unjustifiable. If my house is burning, my rushing into it does not by any means prove that I believe my family is inside; all it shows is that I am aware of the possibility. In a situation allowing more time for conscious reflection (e.g., Mr. Truman and the atom bomb) we would hold a man to be acting irrationally who did not carefully weigh all the available evidence, then act in accordance with the preponderance of probability; but to suppose that deciding to do one thing rather than another is identical with freeing one's mind of

> every doubt—
> All probable, possible, shadow of doubt—
> All possible doubt whatever,[73]

is an outrageous falsification of the process of rational choice. It is advantageous not to dither, but also not to be rash; and any superiority that dogmatists have in the first respect is canceled by their proneness to impulsive behavior and rigid courses of action. If we insist on regarding life as a gambling game, let us not overlook the wisdom of hedging our bets.

The Personal Advantages of Religious Belief

But, it will be said, we cannot hedge our bets on the Deity. The question is, What are we to *do?* We must either *act* on the religious hypothesis, or not. Is it reasonable to have masses said, take holy water, etc.? Or (if this be more efficacious) consult psychologists about how to get rid of doubts?

Let us consider the matter, then, as a practical problem. On the Jamesian assumptions, there is nothing to be said, on balance, either for or against theism, "on intellectual grounds." But theism has all the advantages from the practical side. Whatever may be said, in general, about the ideal of proportioning assent to the degree of evidence, we should not lose sight of the fact that intellectual values are not the only values there are—it would not be reasonable to neglect this. If, then, we are convinced that theists are better off, here and now, than skeptics—more serene, better able to bear up under adversity, less bumbling in action, etc.—is it not obvious that a reasonable man will be confirmed in his belief if he has it;

[73] William S. Gilbert, *The Gondoliers,* Act I.

and if he has it not then will he not try to get it, or—what is easier to effect—to instill it in his children; and will he not lend his support to such public measures as tend to encourage religion?

Indeed, why not? Granting the assumptions of "The Will to Believe," one cannot conclude, logically, that the person who believes in a Deity without evidence *knows* that there is a Deity, even if there is one. "Ignorance is ignorance; no right to believe anything is derived from it."[74] I do not think many people, least of all sincere believers, would quarrel with this verdict of Freud's, if "right to believe" means "right to claim knowledge." One *can* conclude, however, that it is better to be a theist than not to be one.

Better, that is, in the abstract. But if we are to consider the question of what it is reasonable to *do*, the first thing we notice is that it is no good trying to be a theist in the abstract. If the doubter, convinced by James that he should endeavor to get rid of his doubts, sets out to do something about it, the obvious first move is to embrace some particular religion. And at this point he may find that all existing religions are more or less intellectually objectionable, that there is something or other in the creed, to which he is asked to subscribe, that will not go down. It is hard to find an organized sect that demands no more than acceptance of dogmas for which there is no evidence one way or the other; most require what Kierkegaard candidly called "the crucifixion of the intellect."[75] The Jamesian may not want to go that far.

Let us grant, however, that some institutionalized religions, while still officially requiring one to believe "impossible

74 Sigmund Freud, *The Future of an Illusion*, tr. W. A. Robson-Scott (New York: Doubleday Anchor Books), p. 56.

75 I have not succeeded in relocating this formulation of a principal Kierkegaardian *motif*.

things," do not enforce these demands; or even that the Jamesian may encounter a recognized religion whose whole creed amounts to nothing more than the general cosmic optimism which was theism as James evidently understood the term. One becomes a member in good standing if one merely believes—or, perhaps, only hopes—that there exists "a power not ourselves . . . which not only makes for right-eousness, but means it, and which recognizes us"; one is granted to have "faith" if one has "readiness to act in a cause the prosperous issue of which is not certified to us in advance."

This all sounds amiable enough, and one would have to be cantankerous indeed to object to it. Yet it is an oddly pianis-simo conclusion to the pragmatic philosophy of religion—pragmatism that first proclaims, in a blare of trumpets, "There can *be* no difference . . . that doesn't *make* a difference"![76] For it takes sharp eyes to detect any difference between the theist, so defined, and the atheist. To be sure, the latter may reject the plank about the "power not ourselves"; but inso-far as belief in such a power translates itself into action, the result, it would seem, must be a conviction that the power will see to it that everything turns out all right in the long run, i.e., "certifies to us in advance" that all our causes will have "prosperous issues." Hence the only difference between the Jamesian theist and the Jamesian atheist is that the latter has more Jamesian "faith"! The only way to avoid this para-doxical conclusion is to maintain that no atheist can possibly exhibit "readiness to act in a cause the prosperous issue of which is not certified in advance." And this is psychologically preposterous.

But now, what about the allegation that believers are hap-pier than unbelievers? This premise is the shaky foundation of the whole pragmatic argument. As a generalization, it is

[76] James, *Pragmatism*, pp. 49 f.

hardly meaningful, let alone true. We have to ask: Believers in what? Happier in what ways? Perhaps the believer in the attenuated theism of James is always to some degree happier than the man who rejects even that much; but it is not certain, and in any case it would need nice discrimination to show that the increase of serenity (or whatever) derived from it is great enough, either always or for the most part, to make any significant difference in action. Hume's comment on the argument from design surely applies here: "It affords no inference that affects human life, nor can be the source of any action or forbearance." And it is clear that more robust theisms do not always make believers in them happier: consider the terrors of Greek religion, from which Epicurus claimed, with some reason, to have offered deliverance to mankind. Or consider the Phoenician mother, obliged by her belief to cast her first-born into the fiery belly of Moloch, while the drums beat and the cymbals clashed to drown out the screams. Or the dread of hell-fire. It is as well established as anything in history that many men have abandoned their beliefs with a hearty sigh of relief. This is not to deny that some kinds of religion on balance tend to induce euphoria in their devotees. But these religions need to be specified. And in any case, the price paid for that exaltation is never insignificant, either to the individual or to society.

There is something feeble, and a little contemptible, about a man who cannot face the perils of life without the help of comfortable myths. Almost inevitably some part of him is aware that they are myths and that he believes them only because they are comforting. But he dare not face this thought, and he therefore cannot carry his own reflections to any logical conclusion. Moreover, since he is aware, however dimly, that his opinions are not rational, he becomes furious when they are disputed. He therefore adopts persecution, censorship, and a narrowly cramming education as essentials of statecraft. In so far as he is successful, he produces a population which is timid and unadventurous and incapable of progress. Authoritarian rulers have always aimed at producing such a population. They have usually succeeded, and by their success have brought their countries to ruin.⁷⁷

Review of the Jamesian Arguments, and Conclusions

In this section and the one preceding we have presented and discussed two arguments put forth by William James concerning the reasonableness of belief in a Deity. The first is this:

1. True beliefs are beliefs that work.
2. Beliefs that work are beliefs that on the whole and in the long run make their believers happier.
3. Belief in a Deity makes the believer happier, on the whole and in the long run.
4. Therefore belief in a Deity is true.

The second argument (much condensed) is:

1. There is no intellectually compelling basis for deciding whether theistic belief is, or is not, true (in the objective, correspondence sense of "true").
2. But it is not possible to suspend judgment on the question of theism; for doing so would be indistinguishable, in practice, from rejecting it.
3. Therefore the question of theism must be decided, and on other than intellectual grounds.

⁷⁷ Bertrand Russell, *Human Society in Ethics and Politics* (New York and London, 1954), Pt. II, ch. 7; Mentor Books ed., pp. 183 f. Copyright by Bertrand Russell; quoted by permission of the publishers, George Allen & Unwin Ltd., and Simon and Schuster, Inc.

4. The question should be decided favorably to theism, because:

    (a) If there is a Deity, then the theist knows the truth; and

    (b) In any case, theistic belief makes one happier here and now, and by its very nature can never turn out wrong in experience.

5. Therefore it is reasonable to believe in a Deity.

While the first argument is not stated systematically, in any single passage, by James, attributing it to him is not unfair, because all the premises are urged by him, in one place or another, and also because the second argument really reduces to the first when the indefensible premise 4a is removed from it.

"Reasonable," as applied to beliefs, means "in accord with the available evidence"; as applied to actions, it means "calculated to maximize values as far as possible in the situation; expedient." In conformity with these definitions, circumstances might arise in which it would be reasonable (in the action sense) to act on the basis of belief that was unreasonable (in the evidential sense).

One tactic employed in both Jamesian arguments is the redefinition in effect of "reasonable belief" so that as a matter of logic the conflict just noted cannot arise. This is done by making action the sole and conclusive test of belief. But such redefinition is hardly advisable. If we redefine "belief" so that from "he ran into the burning house" we can infer with certainty "he believed that his wife and children were trapped in it," we shall have to invent some other word to signify the actual state of the man's mind, which may have been only one of thinking (or, in the ordinary sense, believing) it possible, though improbable, that they were there. Let this new word be "feileb." Then we can still classify feilebs as rational or irrational, accordingly as they conform to the evidence or not; and it still might happen that a reasonable belief-action was predicated on an unreasonable feileb.

It is best, then, to construe the argument as urging the primacy of reasonable actions over reasonable beliefs—as advising one to *act* reasonably in any case, even if such action necessitates believing unreasonably. And this seems to be sound enough advice. Reasonable belief, though valuable in itself and worth some sacrifices, ought not to be made into an idol on whose altar all other values are to be dedicated. In consequence, both arguments reduce to the question whether or not theistic belief is always, or by and large, productive of greater value *in experience, all things considered,* than lack of it. This knotty question is partly a factual one; and insofar as it is, the answer depends on the particular religion in question, and the psychological make-up of the particular person confronted with the option of adopting or rejecting. It seems safe to say, though, that no one has yet propounded a religious belief that can be guaranteed to make *all* believers happy *all* the time, *all* things considered, on the whole and in the long run.

I have refrained from bringing against these arguments the objection, stated so eloquently by W. K. Clifford (whom readers of James will remember as the great pragmatist's *bête noire*), that we have a *moral* duty to abstain from wishful thinking:

It is wrong in all cases to believe on insufficient evidence; and where it is presumption to doubt and to investigate, there it is worse than presumption to believe.[78]

[78] William Kingdon Clifford, "The Ethics of Belief," in *The Scientific Basis of Morals, and Other Essays* (1884).

For I agree with James that if holding some overbelief makes life happier, on the whole and in the long run, than not holding it; and if the happiness derived from it is not bought at too great expense (such as subconscious conflicts, manifested in tendency to bigotry perhaps; or such as carry-over into a habit of disregarding evidence in matters subject to confrontation with reality)—in short, if someone manages to derive pleasure from a really harmless overbelief, and does not himself suffer or make others suffer in his efforts to convince himself that the belief in question is not really an *over*belief —then why be puritanical about it and try to deprive him of his innocent fun? But though I am no psychologist, I doubt whether these conditions are often fulfilled.

In sum: to our question, Is it reasonable to believe that there is a Deity? we can derive from the arguments of James that we have examined, a partial and heavily qualified affirmative answer. Even if there is no evidence to support the belief, holding it is reasonable—in the expediency sense only— if doing so is pleasant, and if one can manage to keep from consciously recognizing that the belief in question is an overbelief, without thereby debilitating one's intellectual powers of discrimination in general. And it is possible that some persons can do this. In order for them to succeed, though, it is essential that they should not take the pragmatic argument seriously. As far as others are concerned, however, the pragmatic argument fails, on pragmatic grounds. On the whole and in the long run, believing without evidence doesn't work.

Part V

MORAL AND POLITICAL ARGUMENTS

SINCE ancient times it has been contended that regardless of the objective truth of theism, belief in a Deity must be maintained because without it the foundations and effective sanctions of morality are swept away, ordered society collapses, and man is reduced to a state of mere anarchy; or at least because only highly undesirable systems of government are compatible with absence of belief in a Deity among the population at large. Hence it is reasonable (i.e., expedient) to believe in a Deity, and to encourage belief in others. In recent times this argument has tended to receive more emphasis than it formerly enjoyed.

At first look this line of argumentation differs from the pragmatic arguments previously examined only in stressing the social values of religion rather than its worth for the individual. And so it does. But there are, in addition, considerations having to do with the relation of religion to morality that necessitate a more extended treatment of this subject.

For religion, it is urged, is the indispensable basis of morality in one or the other, or both, of two ways: first, only theistic belief can afford a strong enough *motive* for moral behavior, e.g., hope of heaven or fear of hell; second, without theistic belief there can exist no satisfactory objective basis for *distinguishing* right from wrong: no moral law without a supreme lawgiver. These are distinct considerations, though related.

Theism as Providing the Motive

for Moral Behavior

DURING the Middle Ages, it was customary to defend the claims of secular authorities on the ground that "the powers that be are ordained of God." Since the seventeenth century there has been a reversal: it has become more usual to defend religion by arguing that piety is indispensable to good citizenship. Until about three hundred years ago it was also taken for granted that the cohesion essential for a nation-state could be assured only if all the inhabitants thereof subscribed to the detailed creed of the state religion. But because nowadays this argument is no longer advanced except in Spain and the Communist countries, we need consider only the looser claim that agreement on the existence of a Deity of *some* kind is essential to a viable social order: either because fear of God's wrath is the indispensable means for keeping the wicked in check, or (as in Kant's version of the moral argument[79]) be-

[79] Immanuel Kant, *Critique of Practical Reason*, Pt. I, Bk. II, ch. 2, sec. 5.

cause even those who are by nature good will be too discouraged to be effective moral agents if they have no hope of an eventual reward.

Like most types of argument, this one was discovered by the Greeks. The oldest extant statement of it, and still perhaps the most vivid, occurs in the play *Sisyphus*, by Critias the Athenian:

> A time there was when anarchy did rule
> The lives of men, which then were like the beasts',
> Enslaved to force; nor was there then reward
> For good men, nor for wicked punishment.
> Next, as I deem, did men establish laws
> For punishment, that Justice might be lord
> Of all mankind, and Insolence enchain'd;
> And whosoe'er did sin was penalized.
> Next, as the laws did hold men back from deeds
> Of open violence, but still such deeds
> Were done in secret,—then, as I maintain,
> Some shrewd man first, a man in counsel wise,
> Discovered unto men the fear of Gods,
> Thereby to frighten sinners should they sin
> E'en secretly in deed, or word, or thought.
> Hence was it that he brought in Deity,
> Telling how God enjoys an endless life,
> Hears with his mind and sees, and taketh thought
> And heeds things, and his nature is divine,
> So that he hearkens to men's every word
> And has the power to see men's every act.
> E'en if you plan in silence some ill deed,
> The Gods will surely mark it; for in them
> Wisdom resides. So, speaking words like these,
> Most cunning doctrine did he introduce,
> The truth concealing under speech untrue.
> The place he spoke of as the God's abode
> Was that whereby he could affright men most,—

The place from which, he knew, both terrors came
And easements unto men of toilsome life—
To wit the vault above, wherein do dwell
The lightnings, he beheld, and awesome claps
Of thunder, and the starry face of heaven,
Fair-spangled by that cunning craftsman Time,—
Whence, too, the meteor's glowing mass doth speed
And liquid rain descends upon the earth.
Such were the fears wherewith he hedged men round,
And so to God he gave a fitting home,
By this his speech, and in a fitting place,
And thus extinguished lawlessness by laws. . . .
Thus first did some man, as I deem, persuade
Men to suppose a race of Gods exists.[80]

The gods do not exist, but it has been necessary to invent them. Perhaps Critias believed literally that some wise statesman had consciously thought up this clever stratagem for keeping the unruly *polloi* in line; but that is immaterial. Nor does it really matter whether the gods exist or not; the important thing is that people should believe they do. The function of gods—served as well by imaginary gods as by real ones, perhaps even better—is that of celestial auxiliary police. Human laws are sufficient to restrain the beast in man when the police are around—but they cannot be everywhere at once. Hence the stratagem of convincing men that even when earthly police are not watching, the invisible force is right there. There is no cause to doubt the sincerity of Critias when he applauded the shrewdness of the "man in counsel wise" who had this inspiration—though it was not very shrewd of Critias to let the secret be shouted all over the Theater of Dionysus.

[80] In Sextus Empiricus, tr. R. G. Bury (Loeb Classical Library; Cambridge, Mass.: Harvard University Press), III, 31-33; quoted by permission of Harvard University Press, publisher and copyright holder.

It is important to notice that for Critias the criteria of moral judgment, that is, the standards for distinguishing between right and wrong, good and wicked, do not in any way depend on the existence, real or postulated, of gods. These criteria were known by everybody, even "when anarchy did rule"; they are simply the norms of behavior required to make civilized living possible. The gods were not needed in order to inform men about what is right, only to furnish a motive to observe the already recognized norms.

No one would deny that Critias recognized one at least of the important functions of religious belief. Twenty-three centuries later, Freud too acknowledged the crucial role of religious belief in making civilization possible:

Every individual is virtually an enemy of culture, which is nevertheless ostensibly an object of universal human concern. . . . Thus culture must be defended against the individual, and its organization, its institutions and its laws, are all directed to this end. . . . To put it briefly, there are two widely diffused human characteristics which are responsible for the fact that the organization of culture can be maintained only by a certain measure of coercion: that is to say, men are not naturally fond of work, and arguments are of no avail against their passions.[81]

Religion, he goes on to say, has always been one of the major weapons, wielded by the minority who are actively interested in furthering culture, to coerce the slothful and unruly but, fortunately, credulous majority.

Now no one, least of all a believer, should complain about this use of religion. If there are independent reasons for believing that there is a Deity who rewards the virtuous and punishes the wicked, there can be no objection to pointing out the fact, and taking advantage of it to make people be-

[81] Freud, *op. cit.*, pp. 7-8.

have. It must indeed be the will of the Deity that this be done. Nor has the unbeliever cause to be shocked. Even if an avenging Deity is mere myth, objection against the use of the myth cannot be sustained if its use furthers the general interest, if it is more effective for the purpose than available alternatives, and if the undesirable side effects do not outweigh the good it does. Besides, at worst the myth is a noble lie, "the truth concealing under speech untrue": civilized behavior *is* of advantage to everyone concerned, even to the slob who is taken in; but it does no good to tell *him* the truth; "Arguments are of no avail against his passions." Symbolic truth is best for him.

Religion, even when universally believed, has notoriously been unsuccessful in making all men behave morally. But one can always argue that if it had not been for religion, things would have been even worse. And much evidence can be produced in support of this argument. In the fifth century, Rome was sacked first by the Goths and later by the Huns; neither event was pleasant, but the Huns were worse than the Goths, and it is fair to attribute the difference to the fact that the Goths were Christians (though heretical). Czar Nicholas I was for all his faults sincerely devout, and probably that is why he abstained from atrocities and perfidies that did not bother Stalin at all. Let us pass over the Crusades, the suppression of the Albigensian Heresy, the Inquisition, the witch burnings, etc., and concede the past to religion altogether. The question of practical import to us is whether the inculcation of religious belief is an effective and desirable expedient for ameliorating human behavior *today*.

I say the question is that of *inculcation* of religious belief, as it is not likely that anyone is going to say to *himself*, "I now perceive that I will become a more moral person if I believe in a Deity: I will therefore have masses said, take holy water, etc." Since we are discussing a practical question, let us discuss it practically: who would do the inculcating, and how?

If we are talking about the United States, or more broadly the Free World, as it is today, we must take notice of the facts that one may expect current missionary and revivalist activities to continue; that nonbelievers are not going to co-operate actively in this work; that the present campaigns of religious indoctrination are not so effective as might be wished; and that they could be made more effective, in the long run, only if certain measures were adopted. These would have to include religious indoctrination in the public schools; suppression, by law, of opposition to religion as well as of all discussion (such as that in this book) which presupposes that fundamental religious doctrines are arguable; religious tests for public office and private employment; and use of public funds for the encouragement of religion. In short, the *conditio sine qua non* for making everybody religious is now, as it always has been, the active cooperation of the state in the endeavor. And really vigorous support, too, going far beyond mottoes on the currency, public recommendation of church attendance and prayer, pronouncements identifying atheism with Communism, and sporadic, more or less furtive governmental boosts to religion such as exclusion of alien atheists from the country and harassment of soldiers who make no religious declaration on their enlistment forms.

The practical obstacles to implementing such a program, however desirable it may be, are probably insuperable in this country. Not just that a constitutional amendment would be required; perhaps an overwhelming majority of the citizenry are in favor of breaking down the wall separating church and state—in the abstract. But a program such as I have outlined could hardly be carried out without making some *particular* religion the state religion; and to this action one might expect considerable opposition. For indoctrination cannot be effective unless there is some meaty body of doctrine to be instilled; and the common denominator of all religious groups—even just of the dozen or so major ones operating in this country—is notoriously elusive. Besides, some religious bodies, for instance the Unitarians, would be opposed *on religious grounds* to every part of the program.

So much for practical matters. And perhaps that is all that needs to be said. But since we are supposed to be discussing what it would be reasonable to do, if it could be done, let us imagine for a moment some community in which the obstacles I have enumerated do not exist or can be overcome. Would it then be desirable to put such a program into effect? In particular, ought a reasonable and public-spirited nonbeliever to cooperate with it, or at least not actively oppose it?

In the past such programs have been advocated and defended by believers on the ground that since salvation depends on belief, and salvation is the most important thing there is, it is clearly in the interest of everybody to discourage unbelief by every means at his disposal.[82] Such advocacy, if reasonable, depends on knowledge of the existence and intentions of the Deity. We are not now, however, considering this kind of view—though perhaps I may be permitted to say that I can see no valid objection to it, granted its assumption of knowledge. We are now discussing the expediency of religious in-

[82] The Creed of the Council of Trent, 1564, confirmed by Pope Pius IV, and reaffirmed by Pope Pius IX in 1877, concludes: "With the help of God, I shall profess it whole and unblemished to my dying breath; and, to the best of my ability, I shall see to it that my subjects or those entrusted to me by virtue of my office hold it, teach it, and preach it. So help me God and his holy Gospel" (quoted in *The Church Teaches*, p. 9).

doctrination as a means of improving the moral tone of society.

As always when making decisions about what is expedient, we need to determine what is to be got, at what cost. Whether a sharp increase in religiosity, under modern conditions, is likely to result in a substantial decrease in crime, swindling, juvenile delinquency, alcoholism, and immorality of one sort or another, is a question the answer to which must not be taken for granted. No doubt by definition *true* religiosity would have this effect; but we are talking about what would happen if religious *conformity* were imposed, which is all that can be hoped from an intensive campaign. It is a question for elaborate investigation by sociologists. We need data about the behavior of two groups, alike in relevant respects except that one is religious and the other not. If the religious group is significantly "better," the question is answered affirmatively; if not, not. I do not know of any large-scale study of this sort; what little information is available (e.g., the Kinsey investigations, where they bear on sexual "immorality") does not seem to indicate any striking difference. Morality, however that may be defined, appears to be correlated more closely with such factors as social status, income, housing, and level of education than with religious affiliation, or even with intensity and seriousness of religious conviction. In short, it would be surprising if further study were to yield reasons for firm expectation that intensive and successful religious indoctrination of the public would produce a significant lessening of antisocial behavior.

And the cost would be high: thought control. I do not want to maintain that nothing would be worth paying the price of thought control. If by that means it could be brought to pass that everybody should forget how to make nuclear explosives, then I would be in favor of bringing on the inquisitors at once. But it is hardly conceivable that any sober person would be willing to adopt such means just in order to decrease the incidence of crime, even if it were known, as it is not, that the decrease would be drastic.

To sum up: it is not unreasonable for anyone, even an unbeliever, to *wish* that everyone would become devoutly religious, in order that tendencies to moral behavior might thereby be strengthened by the added sanction; it *is* unreasonable for anyone to take the measures required to bring it about.

Theism as Theoretical

Foundation of Morals

THE argument we have just examined tries to establish the necessity of assuming that there is a Deity to act as enforcer of moral rules and regulations. This should not be confused with the contention, which we shall now take up, that moral distinctions *make no sense* unless there is a Deity.

We may say that a man is thirty-seven years old, weighs 160 pounds, and has blue eyes. Such statements have objective reference: their truth or falsity is to be determined by procedures of comparison with external standards: birth records and clocks, scales calibrated against the standard kilogram, colorimeters, etc. Their truth is independent of what anyone thinks or hopes. People may be mistaken about them, and there are objective procedures for detecting such mistakes.

We may also say that the man has a duty to support his family, but has done wrong in swindling widows and orphans for this purpose. Do statements such as these have objective reference? Or rather, we should ask first, are they such as to be either true or false? The presumption is that they are: there is nothing odd about saying, for example, that Jones mistakenly supposes that he has no obligation to support his family. But in these contexts it is not so easy to point to the external standard by which we should justify our judgments. There is no International Bureau of Moral Standards. If people quarrel about the weight of an object, they settle their difference by putting the object on a scale. If the accuracy of the scale is questioned and the matter is of enough importance, the scale can be taken to Sèvres and checked, and that will end the dispute. But if their quarrel is about the morality of divorce, or birth control, or the use of hydrogen bombs to defend Freedom, how is the disagreement to be settled? No doubt "reasons" of one sort or another can be adduced in support of the various views; but ordinarily these are not such as to command general assent.

Reflection on such matters has led some thinkers to proclaim that moral judgments are not really true or false at all, because they are just expressions of feelings. If I say that birth control is wrong, and you say no, it is a duty, we are only expressing, in a misleading fashion, the same information that would be conveyed if I said, "Birth control? O horror!" and you retorted, "Hurrah for birth control!" I am saying that I deplore it, you are saying that you like it, and that is the end of the matter. One feeling is as good as another. If some third person were to say that I am right and you are wrong, we would have nothing but a third expression of feeling. Indeed, we were not really disagreeing in the first place: there was nothing for us to disagree *about*, no objective reference.

This view, that moral judgments have no objective validity but are merely expressions of feeling, either individual or culturally induced, is called ethical relativism. The Carthaginians thought it right to burn the first-born, the Romans thought it wrong. The Roman view prevailed because the Romans exterminated the Carthaginians. And that was the only way it could have been settled, even theoretically. If Hannibal had triumphed, then the burning of the first-born would have been right, i.e., approved of by the survivors. There is no way, ultimately, for settling a moral dispute except by nonrational persuasion or resort to force.

Ethical relativism is to most people an unattractive and implausible theory. We feel (!) that there must be something wrong with it, that in some sense it was in the nature of things wrong for Carthaginians to burn helpless infants, that it is in the nature of things right to keep one's promises, and that it is even more important to have correct views about morals than about "facts."

Now, it is urged, there is a way, and just one way, to avoid ethical relativism. Only if "This is right" means "God commands this," is moral objectivity assured. Right and wrong and the like no longer depend on what we feel; they are imbedded in the nature of things. Two conclusions may be drawn: the first is that we all do, and must, assume that moral judgments are objective (otherwise "anything goes," which is intolerable); in consequence, as a matter of logic we must assume also that there is a Deity. But the conclusion can be presented in a stronger form: since we *know* that moral judgments are objective, we *know* that there is a Deity.

In summary:

1. Either "right" means "commanded by the Deity" or it means "approved of by the speaker"—either theism or ethical relativism.

2. But we cannot, in practice, assume ethical relativism (or: we know that ethical relativism is false).

3. Therefore we must assume that there is a Deity (or: we know that there is a Deity).

Despite its considerable plausibility and popularity, this

argument is very weak. One might counter the second premise by showing that ethical relativism is not such a bogey as it is alleged to be. I have no heart for this task, however, for I think that ethical relativism is demonstrably false. One might also show that the alternation in the first premise is not exhaustive—that there are other tenable theories about the foundations or morals besides theism and relativism. But to show this would necessitate a long discursus. The shortest way to deal with this argument is to show directly that ethical theism is not a tenable theory.

The vitiating flaw, which was in effect pointed out by Plato in the little dialogue *Euthyphro* more than two thousand years ago, is that if "right" simply means "commanded by God," then we cannot say of any right action, X, that God commands X *because* it is right; or if "good" simply means "approved by God," then we cannot even say, "God is good." Or, rather, these statements become trivial. Since we can always substitute the definition for the term defined, "X is right because God commands it" becomes "X is commanded by God because God commands X," and "God is good" becomes merely "God approves of God." Thus God's goodness would be not an independent attribute but would be reduced to the other attributes of power and knowledge—power and knowledge *simply*, not power to produce *good*, or knowledge of *good*. We would be committed to the view that "right" and "good" have no meaning other than "being commanded by, and approved by, a Being of infinite power and knowledge," and there could be no reason why such a Being might command one thing rather than another. If such a Being commanded His creatures to maximize suffering, then suffering as such would become good, and well-being would be evil. It would be just an accident—we could not say a happy accident—that presumably He has not seen fit to do so. To put it another way: on this view, if the Devil somehow acquired God's power, then the Devil would *be* God, and whatever the Devil wanted would be right and good.

Some theologians have not shrunk from drawing this conclusion—which, we should note, is properly to be called theistic relativism. But most have agreed with St. Thomas Aquinas that God's knowledge includes knowledge of what is right and good; in other words, these terms really do have objective reference. That God could not make wanton cruelty right by commanding it is no more a derogation of His power than is the fact that He could not make two and two equal to five. God *recognizes* the right and good as He recognizes the logical. But if God recognizes the good with His intellect, there is no reason why men should not be able to use their reasoning powers to do so also. Ethics no more depends on God than arithmetic does.

This is not to say that theology is altogether irrelevant to morals. It may still be of great practical importance to deciding what is right. Let us take a mundane parallel: suppose I am a poor arithmetician, but my teacher never makes a mistake. Then if I add up a sum and am in doubt about the correctness of the answer, the reasonable thing for me to do is to ask teacher what the right answer is. I may have much better reason for thinking that teacher's answer is right than for trusting my own calculation. But I should not confuse the true statement, "Teacher's answers are always right," with the absurd one, "Teacher's saying so is what makes the answer right." What makes the answer right is inherent in the concepts themselves; my faith in teacher is justified by her superior powers of understanding these concepts.

So also, if we know that there is a benevolent Deity, and, further, we have some means of knowing what He commands, we would be justified in taking His commandments as more reliable indications of the right and the good than our own admittedly imperfect insights—even if these commandments seem to us very strange. For example, if we try to apply our merely human powers of reason to the rights and wrongs of sexual behavior, we may come to the conclusion that relations between consenting adults ought to be left to the judgments of the individuals concerned, unless these individuals are likely to spread disease or produce children whom they will not care for properly. It is well known, however, that persons authorized to relay God's commandments inform us that the true rights and wrongs are altogether different.

We can sum up the conclusions of this part as follows:

1. If there are no compelling reasons, apart from moral and political considerations, for believing that there is a Deity, then:

(a) Moral and political considerations cannot of themselves furnish any compelling reasons for belief.

(b) But it may still be desirable, on account of moral and political considerations, that belief in a Deity should be universal. It is not expedient, however, in the present situation, to institute measures to ensure this conformity of belief.

2. Ethical theory does not presuppose theism; "right" does not mean "commanded by God," though no doubt everything that is right is commanded by God and everything that God commands is right.

3. If there are compelling reasons, apart from moral and political considerations, for believing that there is a Deity, then:

(a) If it is also known that He grants salvation only to believers, then the most stringent measures are justified to ensure a maximum of correct religious belief.

(b) If, furthermore, there are compelling reasons to

believe that His commandments are what they are represented to be by persons who purport to pass them on to us, then knowledge of these commandments is of the utmost practical importance to morality, since what is really right (as the Deity knows it) often diverges most radically from what human reason, applied to problems of conduct, indicates is right.

Epilogue

DOES IT MATTER?

Review of Conclusions

ARE there any reasons for believing in the existence of a Deity, in the sense in which there are or may be reasons for believing in the existence of one's great-great-grandfather, Hengist and Horsa, Himalayan Snowmen, antineutrinos, or a prime number greater than ten billion? As far as I can tell, there are none. Is it nevertheless reasonable to believe that there is a Deity, in the sense that the good consequences of such belief, measured in terms of vitalization of the believer, or social solidarity and patriotism, or what not, will outweigh the disadvantages of perpetuating a belief unsupported by reasons in the preceding sense? This seems to me very doubtful. Is it, then, reasonable, in any sense at all, to believe that there is a Deity? Apparently it is not.

Here and there through this book I have qualified a premise or a conclusion with an "it seems to me . . . " or equivalent expression; but for the most part I have omitted these clauses as unnecessarily tedious. It should be taken for granted that they stand implicitly in every sentence of this book that is not a statement of obvious fact. In the paragraph just above, however, I felt it desirable to write them out, to emphasize that these are the conclusions reached by one individual, who like T. S. Eliot's hippopotamus, is "only flesh and blood":

> Flesh and blood is weak and frail,
> Susceptible to nervous shock;

he (the writer) freely admits and insists on the possibility that he may have overlooked *the* telling bit of evidence, *the* absolutely conclusive argument; somewhere along the line some logical howler may have been committed that invalidates everything.

At the risk of being repetitious, however, I beg leave to say that it would not be at all proper to take advantage of this disclaimer of infallibility by remarking, "Well then, after all is said and done, there is nothing here but mere opinion," and completing the quatrain:

> While the True Church can never fail,
> For it is based upon a rock.[83]

For the question is not what is based on what rock, but whether the foundation is accessible to mortal inspection. Metaphors aside, if somebody, human or superhuman, happens to have access to the Absolute Truth, that fact alone does not make it reasonable for less favored individuals to believe him, unless he can support his assertions with evidence capable of being assimilated into the corpus of ordinary human knowledge. And to say this is not arrogance, but the opposite. Solipsism may be true, the earth may be flat, there may never be a war in which hydrogen bombs are used; but in the present state of human cognition, it is not reasonable to believe any of these things. Notoriously, human reason is imperfect; but I cannot agree with Hume when he says, near

[83] T. S. Eliot, "The Hippopotamus," in *Collected Poems* (New York: Harcourt, Brace & World, Inc., 1936); quoted by permission of the publishers.

the end of the *Dialogues concerning Natural Religion*, that on that account "a person, seasoned with a just sense of the imperfections of natural reason, will fly to revealed truth with the greatest avidity."

Does It Matter Whether

Theism Is Reasonable?

BUT why *not* fly to revealed truth with the greatest avidity? Someone might say, "I agree with everything you have written. I shall go further and ignore your occasional slight qualifications: I say flatly, theism is absolutely irrational. I don't care. I shall go on believing."

A friend has objected to my discussion of mystical "argument," and especially to my saying in one place that if the mystic said such-and-such, "that would not be playing the rational game." "For," said my friend, "mystics don't argue; they haven't any interest in 'playing the rational game.'"

No doubt this is true, of some mystics at least. And if anyone says, "Don't argue with me, arguments are of no interest to me," why, it is only good manners to be quiet. In this book, however, we are discussing doctrines, not individuals, and the question of manners does not arise.

Well, what *can* be said to someone who explicitly rejects reason? One might point out that very likely he does not re-

ject it altogether; he wants evidence that the house he plans
to buy is not infested with termites, he wants his sick children treated by competent physicians rather than by quacks,
etc.; hence he is inconsistent in accepting rational canons in
all spheres of interest save one. But this will not do, for the
obvious retort is that consistency is a rational criterion, which
is just what he is rejecting.

The situation is a queer one. It appears that there is no
possibility of *proving* to the irrationalist that he should not
be irrational, because any proof we might offer would, if
cogent at all, presuppose canons of logic and evidence, and in
consequence would be circular. You cannot checkmate a man
who refuses to play chess.

But refusals to be rational, or to play chess, have consequences, and it is legitimate to point them out. One consequence of a refusal to play chess is that whereas the nonplay-
er, if he likes, may make disparaging remarks about the fu-
tility of chess, he is in no position to take the haughty line
that the players "don't know what real chess is like," and
that the loser in the last game "wasn't really checkmated at
all." And a consequence of refusal to play the rational game
is that the irrationalist is in no position to claim access to a
"higher truth." The rules of the rational game, vague and
imperfect as they may be, are the only procedures we have to
get at the truth, just as the rules of chess are the presuppositions of checkmating.

I shall not pursue this analogy any further, however, because reasoning, after all, is not a game. We do not make up
the rules; they are imposed on us by the nature of things.
Reason does not need to be defended by a circular piece of
reasoning; it is sufficient to point out that the abandonment
of reason is the abandonment of truth. One who finds food
generally distasteful and often unwholesome is not well

advised to give up eating; he will starve, and no "higher nourishment" will sustain him.

If, then, someone says that theism is irrational, but that he does not care, in a sense there is nothing to say to him. We may ourselves think that he should care, but there can be no question of proving to him that he should. On the other hand, it is quite proper to point out to him that he is obliged to accept the consequences, one of which is that his belief must remain a private conviction; he has no warrant to recommend it to anyone else on grounds of truth.[84]

At the same time, it must be admitted that irrationalists are not usually very lonely.

[84] I doubt whether more can or need be said to Tillich and other Neo-Tertullianists. For a different view, see *The Retreat to Commitment*, by William Warren Bartley III (New York: Knopf, 1962).

Does It Matter Whether

God Exists?

THE question is put in all seriousness. Certainly to many persons the existence of God matters more than anything else. I confess that I do not fully understand this phenomenon; in consequence my remarks about it are bound to be naive. I shall try to make them short.

No doubt we all hope that the right will ultimately prevail, that wickedness will be put down in the long run. Belief that there is a cosmic force making for righteousness is, then, belief that the eventual fulfillment of this hope is guaranteed. Hopes are neither rational nor irrational, and a hope of this kind is not fit object for derision or reproach. Far from it.

But what one *does* to bring about the desired state of affairs *is* rational or irrational, praiseworthy or censurable. Now no doubt, as a matter of psychological fact, there are persons who, if they come to doubt the guarantee, would lapse into a quietistic attitude of "nothing anybody does really matters." Perhaps there are others who, secure in the belief of the inevitable victory of good, conclude that it is unnecessary, or even blasphemous, for them personally to do anything calculated to hasten it; and if they were deprived of their conviction, they might wake up and join the battle.

Neither the one party nor the other can claim any logical sanction for their behavior, however; and for the most part institutionalized religions lend them no encouragement. "In God We Trust" is now the official motto of this republic; but not, one hopes, to the exclusion of "Keep your powder dry." If there is a God, He presumably despises those who sit back and let Him do all the work; if there is no God, then it is even more important that the work be done by the only agents capable of doing it.

Perhaps remarks like these leave out of account what is crucial, psychologically, to many: the matter of personal rewards in a hereafter for doing right, and punishments for doing wrong. I doubt whether this kind of motivation is as widespread as it once was; but if it is not, that would seem to be a matter for rejoicing, even (or especially) by the pious. For certainly it is not and never was a worthy motive. Surely the nuns in the hospitals, spending their lives in onerous and disagreeable labors to help suffering humanity, would be insulted if it were suggested that the reason why they do this is that they consider it a good investment with an eye to an eternity of enjoyment. The satisfactions of doing the Lord's work are sufficient unto themselves. But what makes such labor pleasing in the sight of the Lord is its intrinsic character, which it would still have in precisely the same measure whatever the nature of Ultimate Reality happened to be; and performing it out of any motive other than recognition of this intrinsic character would be to miss the whole point. This is not to deny that it is better that worthy deeds should be done from unworthy motives than that they should not be done at all; and as was admitted in the discussion of pragmatism, where only hope of supernatural reward, or fear of punishment, can as a matter of fact function as an effective motive for right action, it is reasonable to encourage such belief. But the religious are surely right in recognizing such tactics as a *pis aller*.

If the only consequences of theistic belief in action were the encouragement of humility and doing good, it would be captious, or worse, to suggest cognitive inadequacies in it. But in fact there are other less happy results. The remark of Count Cavour, "If we did for ourselves what we do for our country, what scoundrels we should be!" has its religious parallel. All too frequently the effect that theistic belief has on a strong personality is to rationalize arrogance and cruelty. "While I personally shrink from doing such-and-such, it is the Lord's command, and I must submit and do as He bids." We need not cite instances of the appalling results.

An ancient insight is that man creates God in his own image:

If cattle and horses or lions had hands, and could draw with their hands and produce works of art as men do, horses would draw the forms of gods like horses, and cattle like cattle, and make their bodies just like the figures they have.[85]

Ancient, but not entirely accurate. The Olympian gods, on the whole, were ordinary Greeks writ large; that was what Xenophanes was complaining about. But one likes to think that the Carthaginian man in the street was not quite so monstrous as Moloch, and that the average Aztec in his private capacity was less bloodthirsty than Huitzilopochtli. Gods of this sort must have been exaggerations of certain facets of character more or less successfully brought under control in everyday life. On the other hand, the God recommended by

[85] Xenophanes, fragment 15.

Xenophanes, "one, supreme among gods and men, and not like mortals in bodily figure or in mind,"[86] and the gods of those religions that have succeeded tolerably in transcending the cruder anthropomorphisms, are conceived as actualizations of human *ideals*. The only sensible way to distinguish between "higher" and "lower" religions is on ethical grounds, according to what emphasis is put on the goodness rather than power of the object of worship. The God of a higher religion does not have those characters that men actually have—even though assigning them to Him would facilitate a more plausible explanation of why the world is as we find it. He has, rather, those characters that men *wish* they had, the pure concentrated essence of what is *best* (though not commonest, or perhaps not even found) in men.

Thus the essential and proper function of God in the higher religions is that of the ideal, something to be aspired to. But for an ideal to function as an ideal, it need not be actual, or embodied or somehow manifested in any existent thing. On the contrary, being tied to the actual is always a disadvantage. For there really is such a thing as moral progress; and this means that the ideal of one period is inadequate as the ideal of another. But when the ideal of a certain period is declared to exist, and the whole conception of piety and aspiration is centered on due obeisance to that Being, with such determinate characteristics as He was declared to have at the inception, the effect is necessarily to shackle moral progress. The history of religions shows that these obstacles can be overcome, but it shows also how painful the process is; and it shows, too, that in all morally progressive periods the institutionalized religions are not aids but obstacles to the rethinking of moral questions. The effect, to be sure, is in some measure compensated for by the fact that objectification of

[86] Fragment 23.

the ideal works the other way also; in periods of retrogression, such as the Dark Ages, and certainly in our own age too in many places, it serves to prevent a lapse into utter barbarism. But that, I think, is all that can be said for it. An existent ideal is an idol.

Index

Index

Index